PROTESTANT
FAITH *in* AMERICA

J. GORDON MELTON

J. GORDON MELTON, SERIES EDITOR

Facts On File, Inc.

PROTESTANT FAITH IN AMERICA
Faith in America

Facts On File, Inc.
132 West 31st Street
New York NY 10001

Library of Congress Cataloging-in-Publication Data

Melton, J. Gordon
      Protestant faith in America / J. Gordon Melton
         p. cm. — (Faith in America)
      Includes bibliographical references and index.
      ISBN 0-8160-4985-8
      1. Protestant churches—United States—History. 2. United States—Church history.
      I. Title. II. Series.

      BR515 .M47 2003
      280' .4'0973—dc21   2003040814

Facts On File books are available at special discounts when purchased in bulk quantities for businesses, associations, institutions, or sales promotions. Please call our Special Sales Department in New York at (212) 967-8800 or (800) 322-8755.

You can find Facts On File on the World Wide Web at http://www.factsonfile.com

Produced by the Shoreline Publishing Group LLC
Editorial Director: James Buckley Jr.
Contributing Editor: Beth Adelman
Designed by Thomas Carling, Carling Design, Inc.
Photo research by Laurie Schuh
Index by Nanette Cardon, IRIS

Photo and art credits: Cover: Lutheran minister, young people at Thanksgiving (AP/Wide World); church (Digital Stock); John Cotton (North Wind Archives). AP/Wide World: 51, 68, 79, 81, 86, 98, 109, 118; Art Resource: 6; Corbis: 11, 36, 45, 71, 72, 103; Courtesy Oberlin College: 61; Courtesy National Council of Churches: 91; Hulton/Getty: 57; North Wind Archives: 20, 22, 25, 32, 40, 54; Stock Montage: 14, 28, 34, 48, 75, 100, 107.

Printed in the United States of America

VB 10 9 8 7 6 5 4 3 2 1

This book is printed on acid-free paper.

CONTENTS

FOREWORD

AMERICA BEGINS A NEW MILLENNIUM AS ONE OF THE MOST RELIGIOUSLY diverse nations of all time. Nowhere else in the world do so many people—offered a choice free from government influence—identify with such a wide range of religious and spiritual communities. Nowhere else has the human search for meaning been so varied. In America today, there are communities and centers for worship representing all of the world's religions.

The American landscape is dotted with churches, temples, synagogues, and mosques. Zen Buddhist zendos sit next to Pentecostal tabernacles. Hasidic Jews walk the streets with Hindu swamis. Most amazing of all, relatively little conflict has occurred among religions in America. This fact, combined with a high level of tolerance of one another's beliefs and practices, has let America produce people of goodwill ready to try to resolve any tensions that might emerge.

The Faith in America series celebrates America's diverse religious heritage. People of faith and ideals who longed for a better world have created a unique society where freedom of religious expression is a keynote of culture. The freedom that America offers to people of faith means that not only have ancient religions found a home here, but that newer forms of expressing spirituality have also taken root. From huge churches in large cities to small spiritual communities in towns and villages, faith in America has never been stronger. The paths that different religions have taken through American history is just one of the stories readers will find in this series.

Like anything people create, religion is far from perfect. However, its contribution to the culture and its ability to help people are impressive, and these accomplishments will be found in all the books in the series. Meanwhile, awareness and tolerance of the different paths our neighbors take to the spiritual life has become an increasingly important part of citizenship in America.

Today, more than ever, America as a whole puts its faith in freedom—the freedom to believe.

Protestant Faith in America

Although no longer the majority nor even the largest segment of America's religious community, Protestants remain arguably the most influential group. As the people who settled the first British colonies along the Atlantic seaboard, they have claimed a certain priority, in part for their continuity with the older Protestant churches of Europe that originated in the 16th-century Reformation, and in part for their role in the American Revolution and the founding of the new nation.

Protestant dominance has been perpetuated by Protestants' association with many of the most influential American families, from whom many prominent political and business leaders have been drawn. Protestant churches also dedicated much of their energy to the building of schools, many now among the most well-known universities in the world, thus ensuring their leadership role in the intellectual realm.

While other religious traditions struggled for space in the new American nation, Protestantism struggled increasingly to deal with challenges to its dominance of the culture and sought new ways to maintain its role in the increasingly pluralistic 20th century. It still struggles with what seem to be opposing wishes. It wants to preserve what it has created in America, while at the same time desires to be relevant to the unique demands of each new generation. It desires to hold on to traditional moral standards, while trying to respond to new ethical situations. It desires to be loyal to the tradition that it has in common with all Christians, while responding to a call for constant reformation. Protestant Faith in America explores this oldest Christian communion in America and how it is still today adapting to a changing world.

— J. Gordon Melton, series editor

INTRODUCTION

Protestant Origins and Beliefs

AMERICA IS GENERALLY THOUGHT OF AS A PROTESTANT CHRISTIAN country. Protestantism has been the major religious force shaping the nation, and slightly more than half of the population currently profess their membership in a church rooted in the original Protestant movement of the 16th century. Almost all of the American presidents and vice-presidents have been Protestants, as are a majority of the country's business and intellectual leaders.

American Protestants can broadly be divided into two groups. First, there are the churches that trace their history to those state-related churches in Europe in the 16th century that launched the Reformation (see page 8) within the Roman Catholic Church and later replaced it as the dominant religious body across Northern and Western Europe. Included in that group are the Lutheran, Reformed, Presbyterian, Congregational, and Episcopal churches. (The Episcopal Church is the American descendant of the Anglican Church founded in England.)

A second group of European Christians broke with the idea of a state-related dominant church in a given country, and organized free churches, that is, denominations unattached to government control. Both groups exist in strength in America. This volume treats the former group, sometimes called the "mainline" Protestant churches. *Baptist and Methodist Faith in America*,

7

PRECEDING PAGE
Historic moment
This 17th-century woodcut shows Martin Luther nailing his "95 Theses" to the door of a church in Wittenberg, Germany. Luther's ideas led to the Reformation and the establishment of the Protestant churches.

by Julie Ingersoll, another volume in this series, treats the latter group, which includes such churches as the Baptists, Methodists, Disciples of Christ, and other evangelical churches.

The Reformation

Through the Middle Ages, virtually all of Western Europe came under the religious authority of the Roman Catholic Church. However, broad changes in the culture—such as the advent of printed books and the resulting spread of knowledge—served to undermine the church's hold on large segments of the population. Not the least of these events affecting church life was the spread of the bubonic plague into Europe in 1347. Within a mere five years, one third of all of Europe's residents were dead. The destructive power of the disease came just as modern national states were arising in Europe to challenge the continental unity heretofore provided by the Catholic faith.

In spite of those changes, through the 15th century Roman Catholicism continued to reflect a spirit of unity shared by most Europeans. The Roman Catholic Church provided the people with religious truth through the office of the pope (the bishop of Rome). The church was a stable organization of bishops who ran dioceses. The Roman church also claimed authority passed to it directly from the first followers of Jesus Christ. Authority was administered through appointed representatives, the bishops, who worked with the bishop of Rome, and whose word was law within their own diocese.

As the church developed, it brought people into a total relationship with the spiritual world through seven sacraments. These were dramatic ceremonies that presented God's reality of salvation to the believer. Soon after beginning life, a person was baptized and at the end of life, one experienced a final forgiveness of sins. Daily life was anchored in the Eucharist (see the box on page 9), which was the celebration of the main truth of Christianity—that Jesus came to the world to save humanity.

While the Roman Catholic Church supplied a wide-ranging spiritual and religious vision for Europe, all was not well. During the centuries immediately preceding the Reformation, many people felt that corruption had entered almost every level of church life. The priesthood was being undermined by attempts to buy high church offices (a practice called simony) and violations of vows by the clergy to lead a celibate life. As the church became the controlling religious presence throughout all of Europe, it also picked up and integrated into its daily life a spectrum of local and regional folklore. Among the most criticized of practices was the acceptance and circulation of reputed relics of Christ, the Apostles, and other saintly people. Some endowed these relics with almost magical powers, while many dismissed them as objects of popular superstition. Church leaders attempted to correct some of these problems by holding a number of church-wide councils at which reforms were introduced.

The level of discontent continued to grow, however, and at the beginning of the 16th century the unhappiness with the church became focused in the building of St. Peter's, the massive cathedral in Rome (now Vatican City) that would become the new spiritual center of the church. To build St. Peter's, funds were raised across Europe. In popular practice, and with the approval of the pope, church leaders were commissioned to offer what were termed "indulgences" as an incentive to giving toward the erection of St. Peter's.

Catholics saw themselves as engaged in a life-long process of becoming holy, though few succeeded in their lifetime. Most believers

EUCHARIST

It is Roman Catholic belief that during the Eucharistic ceremony the invisible essence of the bread and wine that believers share is transformed into the very body and blood of Christ, while to all outward appearances, they remain bread and wine. This belief is called transubstantiation.

Christianity: The Basics

Protestantism affirms those beliefs of the ancient Christian church that are shared by all Christians, most especially the Roman Catholic Church and the Eastern Orthodox Churches. These beliefs are summarized in several creeds, or statements of belief, most notably the Apostles Creed and the Nicene Creed. The creeds are included in the liturgies of the various churches and repeated by Christians as part of their weekly worship services. They all affirm a belief in:

- **God as a Trinity of Father, Son, and Holy Spirit.** The one God manifests as a loving Father who cares for his creation and human family, the son of God who came into human life to save us, and the Holy Spirit who is God's continuing presence in our lives.

- **The Lordship of Jesus as the world's Savior.** Christians affirm that God became human in the person of Jesus of Nazareth, who died for humanity's sin.

Through his resurrection from the dead, he opened the door for human salvation.

- **The Holy Spirit is God invisibly present in the world and in human hearts.** The Holy Spirit gives life and ensures our relationship with the divine. The Holy Spirit is especially present in the universal Church.

- **The afterlife.** Christians look forward to a future life beyond bodily death in a world to come.

assumed that after death they would have to spend some time in a place called purgatory where the process of attaining holiness continued at an accelerated rate. The experience of purgatory would include punishment for one's sins, and it was not a place one looked forward to visiting. However, it was also the belief that acts of goodness and piety done in this life shortened one's time in purgatory. In addition, the church could also grant indulgences, pardons that would reduce or even eliminate the time in purgatory, either for oneself or a loved one. Early in the 16th century, the church authorized the granting of indulgences to those who contributed to the new building project. Critics of St. Peter's saw the practice as a further sign of the church's corruption.

Martin Luther's Bold Move

A significant challenge to the selling of indulgences began in Wittenberg, Saxony (part of what is today Germany), in 1517, when a young monk, Martin Luther (1483–1546), a professor of theology at the local university, challenged the practice, as well as several other questionable practices and beliefs within the church. He posted a list of 95 contrary theses (debating points) on the door of the church in Wittenberg.

The "95 Theses" reflected a new approach to Christian living he was then developing. This new perspective became more widely available when he was called to account for himself before various church hearings. He also published several pamphlets in 1520. As a result of the pamphlets, he was called before the Diet (legislature) in session at Worms (a city in Germany) to speak before the Emperor of the loosely-organized Holy Roman Empire, which was the primary political structure at the time.

At the Diet, Luther defended his approach. When it was demanded that he recant, he replied that he could do so only if his position were proved wrong by either reference to the Bible or by logical argument. Though condemned as a heretic, he found protection from the ruler of Saxony. His refusal to back down in the face of both secular and religious pressure unleashed a wave of supportive protest across Northern and Western Europe. What began as a questioning of some specific practices quickly became a movement offering a broad critique of Roman Catholicism. Eventually a new form of Christianity, Protestantism, emerged as an alternative.

RELIC

A relic is some part of the bodily remains—bones, teeth, hair, etc.—of a saint or holy person. These remains were sometimes put on display or housed in special tombs, becoming objects of devotion to followers.

Protestant history might have been quite different had it not been for the fact that at about the same time as Luther's protest, the attention of the Holy Roman Emperor was distracted by the Turkish army. Turkish forces had invaded from the east and stood at the gates of Vienna and threatened to overrun central Europe. While the emperor was busy fighting the Turks, Protestants were able to consolidate their strength in those countries most favorable to its new approach. Protestantism became the dominant Christian tradition in Scandinavia, northern Germany, the Netherlands, Switzerland, and the British Isles. It also developed significant followings in other places, including France, Hungary, and Poland.

It should be noted that while Protestantism was united in its opposition to Catholicism, Protestants disagreed among themselves on a variety of issues and as the movement spread from country to country, several different forms emerged, the primary ones being Lutheran, Reformed/Presbyterian, and Anglican.

The Lutherans

Luther emerged as a traditional Christian thinker in many ways. He accepted the basic beliefs of Christianity, and primarily directed his followers' protest at what he saw as relatively new practices and emphases within the Roman Catholic Church, especially the elaborate sacramental system that the church had evolved. For example, Protestants downplayed the role of the priest as the official who facilitated a person's contact with God. Luther argued for the priesthood of all believers and their ability to relate to God without the assistance of a priest. He also attacked the celibacy required of the priesthood.

Luther on the Priesthood of All Believers

Here is what Martin Luther wrote concerning the idea of all Christians being part of the "priesthood" (as quoted in Leslie Dunstan's 1961 book *Protestantism*):

> *Thus we are all consecrated as priests by baptism, as St. Peter says: "Ye are a royal priesthood, a holy nation" (I Peter ii:9); and in the book of Revelations: "and hast made us unto our God, kings and priests" (Rev. v:10). For, if we had not a higher consecration in us than Pope or bishop can give, no priest could ever be made by the consecration of Pope or bishop; nor could he say the mass, or preach, or absolve. Therefore the bishop's consecration is just as if in the name of the whole congregation he took one person out of the community, each member of which has equal power, and commanded him to exercise this power for the rest; in the same way as if ten brothers, coheirs as king's sons, were to choose one from among them to rule over their inheritance; they would, all of them, still remain kings and have equal power, although one is ordered to govern.*

Luther based his new opinions upon his reading of the Scripture, and he denounced beliefs and practices within the church that he saw as contrary to the teachings of the Bible. Against the traditions that had emerged in the church, he called upon Catholic leaders to accept the authority of the Bible alone as the arbiter of their differences. With the recent invention of moveable type and the modern printing press, he was able to publish his views abroad. He also translated the Bible into German and saw popular editions printed. The belief in "sola scriptura," the Bible only, remains a hallmark of Protestant faith.

Luther saw indulgences and the elaborate sacramental system of his day as constituting a process of salvation by works. In contrast, Luther believed that Christians could not work for their salvation; salvation could only be granted as a free gift by God. God alone by his grace could provide salvation to the faithful and nothing the individual does could earn God's favor. The Protestant doctrine of salvation by grace alone through faith became the major divide between Protestants and Catholics.

Over the next years, as Luther's support was consolidated, one of his followers, Philip Melanchthon (1497–1560) wrote and published a lengthy manifesto of the Lutheran position. It was published as the *Augsburg Confession* (1530), still the major statement of the Lutheran perspective. One sees in it the basic Lutheran approach of attempting to rid the church of all elements that they believed were unscriptural. Included was the Catholic doctrine of transubstantiation, which was seen as both unscriptural and bordering on magic. Lutherans replaced it with an affirmation of the real and substantial presence of Christ in the Eucharist, but in such a way that no mystical transformation was performed. Luther called his new idea consubstantiation.

The Reformed Church

As the Lutheran position took hold in Germany, other centers of discontent with the Catholic Church emerged, most notably in Switzerland. Early efforts toward reformation were initiated in German-speaking Zurich by the local priest Ulrich Zwingli (1484–1531). However, the more substantial work was carried out in French-speaking Geneva by John Calvin (1509–1564). In 1536, Calvin, who had been trained as a lawyer, published *The Institutes of the Christian Religion*, the first systematic book-length presentation of the Protestant position.

Another agent of change
Swiss theologian John Calvin adopted some of Luther's ideas, but also added many of his own. He and his followers started what became the Reformed and Presbyterian churches. This 1861 woodcut is modeled on an 18th century painting by Dutch artist Christaan Dankertz.

While he agreed with Luther on most issues, he developed some unique emphases. For example, he began with the sovereignty of God, a doctrine with which Luther agreed, but Calvin so emphasized it that he also came to believe in humanity's utter worthlessness before God. That being the case, individuals could only be saved by an act of God's will, based on the death and resurrection of Christ. Obviously, in looking around, not everyone was living as a Christian should and hence did not show any sign of God's grace. The logic suggested that God had chosen some people for salvation and was leaving the rest to the just results of their evil ways.

Also, Calvin reasoned, since God was all wise and all knowing, He must have predetermined who the elect would be. Those who experienced salvation had thus been predestined to this path. Within the larger world of Protestantism the belief in the sovereignty of God and predestination of some people to salvation would become the distinguishing beliefs of Reformed (and in England, Presbyterian) Christians.

On several occasions representatives of the Lutheran and Reformed churches attempted to work out their differences; they failed and the followers of Luther and Calvin went their separate ways. In the end, what divided them could be most clearly seen in their different approaches to the sacraments, to running the church, and to their interpretation of biblical authority. Luther had, for example, taught the doctrine of consubstantiation, in which he affirmed that Christ truly was present in the Eucharist. Calvin on the other hand, had a much different approach, believing that Christ was not substantially present in the Eucharist but was only spiritually present and could only be perceived by the eye of faith. This argument about the sacrament reflected another difference. Lutherans tend to see the world more mystically while Calvinists have a much more earthly outlook.

This more secular Calvinist approach led to changes in church buildings and in worship services. Lutherans had adopted as their guiding principle the abandonment of beliefs and practices found to be contradictory to the Bible. The Reformed and Presbyterian Churches adopted a more radical approach. They wanted to keep only those aspects of church life that were directly supported in the Bible.

This stricter approach had its most visible effect in the way each treated church buildings. Calvinists demanded that statues and other church ornaments no longer in use be removed, and a more simple and orderly worship become the standard of the day. Also, while Lutherans were not particularly concerned about the symbolic clothing worn by priests while leading worship, Calvinists said such clothing (vestments) were not supported by scripture and they were abandoned.

Calvin reorganized the church. He found no support for the office of bishop in the Bible; rather he saw churches led by elders, or presbyters. In place of a bishop, the Reformed churches designated some members as elders, some of whom operated as teaching elders (ordained ministers) and some as temporal elders (lay people who collectively managed the practical side of church life).

As the movement inspired by Calvin's work in Geneva and his massive tome, *The Institutes of the Christian Religion*, spread, the Calvinists in Continental Europe became known as the Reformed church (emphasizing the reformed theology of the Institutes). Like the Lutherans, the Calvinists drew up several manifestoes (called confessions) that summarized their faith, the most important being the Belgic Confession (1561), and the First and Second (1566) Helvetic Confessions of Faith.

In Scotland and England, the Calvinists became known as Presbyterians, a reference to their reorganization into presbyteries headed by elders/presbyters. The Reformed Church found its greatest strength in Switzerland and the Netherlands. The Presbyterian Church was established in Scotland in the 1560s. Calvinism also spread to France, Hungary and Transylvania (today a part of Romania), parts of Germany, and to a lesser extent elsewhere.

The Special Case of England

At the time the Reformation was building in Germany and Switzerland, England was ruled by King Henry VIII (1491–1547). A staunch Roman Catholic, he wrote a book on the seven sacraments in 1521, for which the pope honored him with the title "Defender of the Faith." However, as king, Henry had nonreligious problems that would eventually drive him from the Catholic Church. First, he saw it as his duty to produce a male heir who would follow him on the throne. His first wife, Catherine of Aragon, produced only one child that survived infancy, a girl named Mary. Henry then decided on a plan to have his marriage annulled and marry someone who could produce a male heir.

When the pope refused to annul the marriage, Henry set about subjecting the Christian community in England to his control, which he accomplished in 1533. He then forced the Archbishop of Canterbury, the leading clergyman in the country, to annul his marriage. He subsequently married Anne Boleyn (c.1500–1536), who gave birth to his daughter Elizabeth in 1533. The next year Henry was declared the supreme head of the Church of England. Without changing any essential doctrines, he in effect broke with the Roman Catholic Church.

Henry's second problem was money, and to solve it he turned to the large, well-established monasteries and convents, home to many monks and nuns across England. In order to refill his treasury and to prepare for a war with his first wife's relatives, Henry took over the monastery properties and their incomes.

Unfortunately, Anne Boleyn proved unable to produce a male child, was charged with adultery, and beheaded. Henry then married a third time, and his third wife, Jane Seymour (1509–1537), finally bore a son, Edward, the future king Henry so wanted.

Though Henry had broken with Rome, he had no use for Protestants and provided few openings for them to assume any positions of influence in England. Quietly, however, Protestant sentiments spread among the people at court and some Protestants became very influential after Henry died and his nine-year-old son became king as Edward VI (1537–1553). During Edward's brief reign, the country was essentially led by a small group of Protestants who served as his guardians and tutors. They tried to move the country into the Protestant camp.

British and American history would have been significantly different had Edward lived past his 15th birthday. However, he died in 1553 and was succeeded by his sister Mary (1516–1558). The youthful Mary immediately began to move England back into the Roman Catholic fold. She became known for the brutality of her regime in which a number of Protestants were executed. Her enemies labeled her "Bloody Mary."

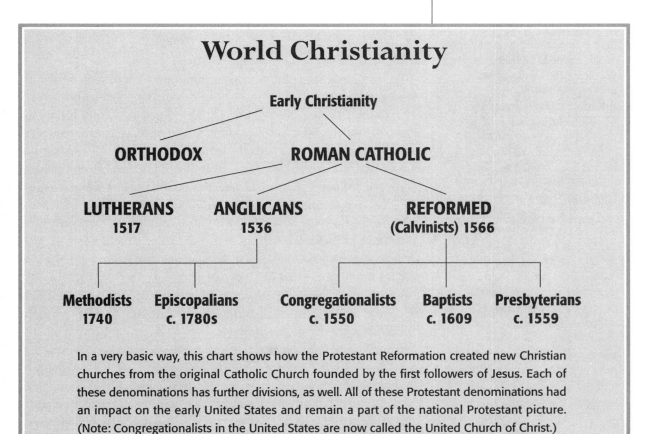

World Christianity

Early Christianity

ORTHODOX　　　**ROMAN CATHOLIC**

LUTHERANS　　**ANGLICANS**　　　**REFORMED**
1517　　　　　　1536　　　　(Calvinists) 1566

Methodists　**Episcopalians**　　**Congregationalists**　**Baptists**　**Presbyterians**
1740　　　c. 1780s　　　　　c. 1550　　　c. 1609　　c. 1559

In a very basic way, this chart shows how the Protestant Reformation created new Christian churches from the original Catholic Church founded by the first followers of Jesus. Each of these denominations has further divisions, as well. All of these Protestant denominations had an impact on the early United States and remain a part of the national Protestant picture. (Note: Congregationalists in the United States are now called the United Church of Christ.)

Elizabeth I Makes Her Mark

Mary's death in 1558 set the stage for the coronation of Elizabeth I (1533–1603), the daughter of Anne Boleyn. One of the truly great leaders of Western history, Elizabeth set to work on the major problem facing Britain at the time—the division between Roman Catholicism and Protestantism in the country. Over the next five years she created a new religious practice that brought together elements of both traditions and left some room for individual differences in belief and practice. She issued a new statement of church beliefs, the Thirty-Nine Articles of Religion, and a new Prayer Book, the book guiding worship in the Church of England. The *via media* (middle way), as Elizabeth's new way was called, became the distinctive perspective of the Anglican (British) church. The church was led by bishops, but its doctrine tended toward the Protestant interpretation.

The Puritans

Elizabeth's new way did not make everyone happy, though outwardly it was imposed upon the church and initially received a high level of compliance. Once people experienced the new way in practice, the Protestants demanded that further purification of the church was needed. They received little sympathy from Elizabeth, they did not begin to have a real voice in moving the country until the next century. However, in the decades following Elizabeth's death, the Puritan movement emerged in force in England. Like the Protestants a century earlier relative to the Catholic Church, the Puritans agreed that the Church of England was in need of further transformation. They disagreed, however, on the nature of the needed changes, and that disagreement would divide them into several distinct camps.

The first group, which emerged under Elizabeth, wished simply to remove a few of the remaining Roman Catholic elements from the church. More importantly, however, they wished to improve life in the many parishes. For example, they wanted the appointment of a capable minister in every parish, and they sought help in improving the spiritual life of the church, too long caught up in royal politics.

A second group, the Presbyterians, wanted much more change. They demanded the elimination of the bishops. Many of those advocating this perspective had been banished during the reign of Mary and had spent their time in Geneva with the Calvinists. They began to advocate replacing the bishops with elders. They drew significant inspiration from their Scottish colleagues who had successfully gotten rid of the bishops and totally reformed the Church of Scotland.

Still a third group, with an even more extreme (for the time) position, also emerged, the Independents. They did not wish so much to tamper with the Church of England as to replace it. They rejected the idea of an established Church in England, an inclusive church tied to the state and dominating the religious landscape. Rather, the Independents wished to create a smaller church made up only of those people who had a lively relationship with God and wished to live a religious life. They came to believe, from their reading of the Bible, that the proper base of authority in the church was neither bishops nor the presbyters, but the congregations.

Between the Presbyterians and the Independents, another group, the Congregationalists, also emerged. Like the Independents, they argued that the primary authority of the church was to be found in properly constituted congregations. In contrast with them, however, they saw no need to sever ties with the state. They hoped the Church of England would reorganize as a Congregational fellowship.

In 1611, the Puritans presented their first accomplishment, a new contemporary translation of the Bible, to the king, James I (1566–1625), who became the ruler of England following the death of Elizabeth. To get the king's approval, knowing his Catholic sympathies, they dedicated it to him, and to this day it is known as the King James version of the Bible.

By the time the European nations began to establish and nurture colonies along the Atlantic coast of what is now the United States, no less that six Protestant groups had emerged in Europe. As the British and others developed settlements along the Atlantic seaboard of North America, members of each group moved to what is now the United States. And so, in the early 1600s, Lutheran, Reformed, Anglican, Presbyterian, Congregationalist, and Baptist congregations were planted on America soil. It is their story that will unfold in the chapters to follow.

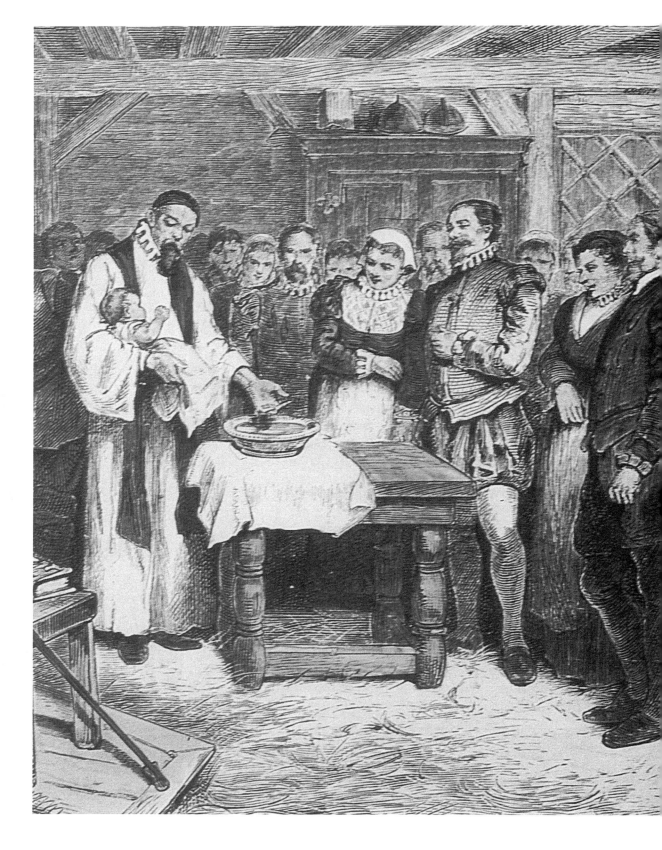

Establishing Protestant Faiths in America

IN 1612, THE COLONISTS WHO HAD RECENTLY SETTLED ALONG THE shores of Virginia were witness to the first of what would in future centuries become a more common event. One of their younger neighbors, John Rolfe (1585–1622), had decided to wed. The marriage would not have been so unique, but for the fact that he had decided to take a young Native American woman, a mere teenager, as his bride. Just four years previously, Pocahontas (c.1595–1617) had saved another colonist from being executed by her father, Chief Powhatan. And now, her wedding to Rolfe would cement a fragile peace between her people and the white invaders.

The very young Pocahontas had come to live at the Jamestown settlement and had converted to the Anglican church, a fact that made her marriage a possibility, but still the pious Rolfe had to listen to the warnings of some townspeople about the biblical injunctions against marrying "strange wives." However, he was in love, and had come to believe that his marriage would be good for the colony. Happily ever after for the couple was only five years—she died of smallpox. But in that time, this early convert to the Christian faith became the stuff of legends (and movies).

The Pocahontas story is remembered partly because it focuses on the good moments of European and Native American interaction in the Colonial

Early English friend
This illustration from a 1907 issue of the magazine Harpers' Weekly *shows Pocahontas and her son Thomas dressed in European-style clothing. The Native American woman played a key role in early colonial relations.*

PRECEDING PAGE
First baptism
This late-19th-century illustration shows the baptism of Virginia Dare in 1587. The young English girl was the first European to be born and baptized in the English colony of Virginia.

era. All too frequently, relations were marred by the European encroachment on Native American land, with rising tensions leading to open conflict. Several years after Pocahontas's death, Rolfe would himself be killed in a battle with his wife's people in 1622. The ongoing tensions between the white settlers and the Native American residents and their very different ideas about life would form the backdrop of the rise of Protestantism in the British colonies.

Anglicanism

The Church of England extended its reach to what is now America in 1587 when some 100 men, women, and children settled on Roanoke Island, off the coast of Virginia. One of the first events they recorded was the birth (which would have soon been followed by the baptism) of a child, Virginia Dare (August 18, 1587). Soon afterward, the leader of the colony, John White, went to England for further supplies. His return to Virginia was delayed by events in England (war with Spain), and when he did arrive, he found no one alive at the colony. Apparently they had been killed by hostile Native Americans.

Thus it would not be until 1607 that worship according to the order of the Church of England would be permanently established in America, with the arrival at Jamestown of a group of settlers under the auspices of the Virginia Company of London. Their sponsor obviously hoped to turn the adventure into a profit for investors, but its charter also stated as among its goals to establish Christianity according to the standards of the Church of England and to engage in missionary activity. Accompanying the colonists was Robert Hunt, an Anglican clergyman. He held the first service for the colonists on May 14, 1607, and repeated the act daily for the duration of his ministry (the date of his death is unknown). The first permanent building erected by the colonists was a crude church, in which in 1608 Hunt performed the first wedding in the colony.

As the colony expanded, Hunt's far more well-known colleague, Alexander Whitaker, arrived in 1611 to become the pastor of the new parish at Henrico. Among the early tasks performed by Whitaker was the baptism of Pocahontas and her subsequent marriage to Rolfe.

Anglicanism was officially the established religion of the expanding colony of Virginia, but religion plainly took second place to the profits desired by the Virginia Company of London, whose money had seeded the settlement and whose investors expected a return. As settlement spread, Anglican churches were founded and ministers sought in England to supply them. Unfortunately, those who accepted the call to America were not always, like Whitaker, the best qualified, and some Anglicans would later complain that only the dregs of the clergy left their more civilized parishes for the New World.

For many decades, Virginia was the only Anglican colony, Maryland having been settled by Roman Catholics and New York by the members of the Reformed Church. Further expansion was slowed by problems in England, where the Catholic sympathies of King Charles I (r.1625–1649) kept the country in turmoil, culminating in Civil War and the establishment of a Puritan Commonwealth under Oliver Cromwell (1599–1658). Virginia's sympathies were plainly with Charles and the settlers welcomed the restoration of the monarchy in 1660.

In 1664, during the reign of Charles II (r.1660–1685), British forces pushed the Dutch out of New Amsterdam (immediately renamed New York) and established Anglicanism in the city. As the British gained authority over the other colonies (from Maine to Georgia), they attempted to establish the Church of England, and while legally successful in most colonies (except New England), nowhere was the establishment very strong. The number and quality of clergy was lacking. Everywhere they faced disagreements from the Puritans, the Baptists, and especially in Pennsylvania, from the Quakers. As the church grew, it was severely hampered by the refusal of the Church in England to send a bishop to the colonies.

In the Anglican tradition (as in Catholicism), the bishop holds the power to ordain ministers and confirm youth as full members. With no bishop, all clergy had to be drawn from England, and colonists were stuck with what ministerial leadership it could get from the mother country. With no bishop, the youth could never be confirmed, unless they traveled to England at some point in their lives. Children growing to adulthood could never become full members of the church (though most ministers ignored their lack of confirmation), and this alienated many who might have become strong church workers. No less a personage than future president George Washington regularly attended church services, but never took communion.

Some help came to the church with the appointment of commissaries, ministers who could exercise some Episcopal authority (though neither ordination nor confirmation). One of these, Thomas Bray (1656–1730), appointed in 1696, became aware of many of the problems faced by those who might consider going to the distant colonies. Prospective ministers had the idealism but were too poor to purchase a library and American parishes were too poor to pay them a proper salary. Bray took the lead in helping establish two organizations to remedy the situation—the Society for the Promotion of Christian Knowledge to publish cheap editions of needed books; and the Society for the Propagation of the Gospel in Foreign Parts (SPG) to recruit missionaries.

However, in spite of the development of the church under the SPG missionaries, no bishop was ever appointed to build the work. If the truth be told, however, as the decades passed, more and more colonists opposed the arrival of a bishop who even the Anglicans believed would be just another instrument of British government tyranny. The New England Congregationalists, of course, absolutely opposed the presence of an Anglican bishop in the colonies. Thus the Church of England in America limped toward the decisive years of the Revolution.

WASHINGTON'S RELIGION

Future Episcopal bishop William White was George and Martha Washington's pastor during the years that the American government had its capital in Philadelphia. Reflecting on this time, he wrote in an 1835 letter, "In regard to the subject of your inquiry, truth requires me to say, that general Washington never received the communion in the churches of which I am the parochial minister. Mrs. Washington was a regular communicant."

The Pilgrims of New England

The story of the coming of Christianity to New England is tied up with some of the most revered symbols in American history—the Mayflower, Plymouth Rock, the first Thanksgiving, and, of course, America's first love triangle: John Alden, Miles Standish, and Priscilla Mullins. The Pilgrims were the first group of Christian believers to come to New England. This small group had originated in Scrooby, a little community in Nottinghamshire (the area of England made famous centuries earlier as the home of Robin Hood). Having given up any hope that the Church of England would further reform and being always under threat of persecution, in 1606 the members of the Scrooby congregation established themselves as an independent body. Three years later they moved to Holland, at the time much more tolerant of diversity than England.

Life in Holland had its own problems, not the least being that their children began to speak Dutch rather than English. Thus, in 1620, many

Time for church
This 19th-century woodcut imagines what a Puritan church service in colonial New England looked like. A minister at a pulpit led the congregation—men, women, and children—in prayer.

of the Scrooby group jumped at an offer from some English merchants to create a colony in Virginia. However, their ship, the *Mayflower,* landed at Cape Cod in what is now Massachusetts, and the Pilgrims decided to stay. They had had enough of the sea, but before stepping foot on land, made a covenant among themselves. Among other things, they agreed to work for the group welfare rather than their individual success.

The obstacles the Pilgrims faced in creating their new life and the manner they chose to overcome their situation are in and of themselves enough to guarantee their place in pioneer history. They braved the winter, built the first houses, and learned to deal with their Native American neighbors. It is not surprising that they became the stuff from which legends were later made. In the spring, they were befriended by two Native Americans who had encountered fishermen and learned English. One, Squanto, had even traveled across the Atlantic, studying in England and then later being captured into slavery in Spain. In the colony, he taught the Pilgrims farming and the other skills they needed to survive. When the first harvest came in mid-October 1621, Governor William Bradford proclaimed a day of thanksgiving and the Pilgrims invited their neighbors to join them for a three day celebration. Our annual holiday has its roots in that first Thanksgiving Day.

Here Come the Puritans

The Pilgrims had Massachusetts largely to themselves for a decade, but in 1620 were joined by a much larger group of believers from England. The Puritans were determined to create their ideal of the godly society headed by Christian magistrates and worthy ministers. Unlike the Pilgrims, whose church was separate from the local government, the Puritans created a society in which church and government worked together in harmony. Here they could purify the Church in ways that Queen Elizabeth and her successors had prevented in England.

When the first wave of 1,000 Puritans landed in Massachusetts Bay, they completely overwhelmed the 300 Pilgrims in Plymouth, and over the next decade their number would grow 20-fold. Puritans spread across present-day Massachusetts and Connecticut and soon formed four separate colonies. Their life developed around a series of covenants. Their salvation, it was believed, was based on God's covenant with humankind. Each church member, as they joined, signed a covenant that committed them to God and the other church members.

Famous Puritan Love Story

We actually know very little of John Alden and the pious Priscilla Mullins, beyond the fact that two such people lived at Plymouth. We know a little more of the soldier Miles Standish, but not much. More than 200 years later poet Henry Wadsworth Longfellow (1807-1882) lifted them from obscurity to tell his story of two friends who loved the same woman. Their friendship was put to the test by Standish's request to the bookish Alden to assist him with his courtship. In the end, Alden won Mullins, and Standish overcame his initial anger to reaffirm his friendship. Here is an excerpt from Longfellow's 1858 poem, *The Courtship of Miles Standish*.

> So through the Plymouth woods John Alden went on his errand;
> Crossing the brook at the ford, where it brawled over pebble and shallow,
> Gathering still, as he went, the May-flowers blooming around him,
> Fragrant, filling the air with a strange and wonderful sweetness,
> Children lost in the woods, and covered with leaves in their slumber.
> "Puritan flowers," he said, "and the type of Puritan maidens,
> Modest and simple and sweet, the very type of Priscilla!
> So I will take them to her; to Priscilla the May-flower of Plymouth,
> Modest and simple and sweet, as a parting gift will I take them;
> Breathing their silent farewells, as they fade and wither and perish,
> Soon to be thrown away as is the heart of the giver."

Their goal was to build a Christian Commonwealth in which faith in God and a godly social order prevailed. Church members had to accept the church's teachings, but also had to offer a public testimony about how they had been saved by God. Once they had been accepted in the church, the men could vote in the elections for government officials. Thus were church and state joined. Together they worked for the establishment of godly order and on those occasions in which church disputes arose, the secular government could step in to make decisions.

Unlike the Anglicans to the south, in their four colonies, the Puritans were able to create a strong religious establishment. They were able to and did react to any dissent that they felt would destroy the faith of the majority, and were quick to suppress those who tried to introduce any unacceptable opinions. The usual punishment was exile from the colony and such was the fate of Anne Hutchinson (see the box on page 28) and the minister Roger Williams (later to found the colony of Rhode Island, where dissenters were freely received). When the first Quakers arrived in Boston from England, they were arrested and run out of the colony. Later arrivals were whipped and fined, and when that did not keep them out, in 1659 several were executed.

The break in the Puritans' exclusive control of the religious life of Massachusetts came only with the arrival in 1687 of a new royal governor, Edmond Andros, an Anglican. He moved quickly to find a place for Anglican services and forced the sale of land upon which the next year the construction of King's Chapel would begin.

The Case of Anne Hutchinson

In 1637, Anne Hutchinson (1591–1643), the wife of one of Boston's leading citizens, was charged with heresy (speaking against church teachings) and banished from the Massachusetts Bay Colony. A woman of learning and great religious conviction, Hutchinson challenged the Puritan clergy and asserted her view of the Covenant of Grace, which essentially said that what was in a person's heart was more important than their moral conduct and piety.

While her trial (right) was about religion, the real confrontation was over the role of authority in the colony. Hutchinson was an outspoken woman in a male-dominated society. At her trial one of her accusers said Hutchinson acted more like a husband than a wife, and more like a preacher than a hearer.

Seventy-five men of Boston had protested the final verdict. The magistrate ordered these men to sur-

render their weapons or to acknowledge that they had sinned in their protest. All surrendered their weapons, but only 35 acknowledged that they had erred in supporting Hutchinson.

Hutchinson moved her family to Rhode Island in the spring of 1638, where she continued to teach and preach. But by 1642 the Massachusetts Bay Colony had grown so large that it threatened to take in other colonies, so Hutchinson and her children moved to what is present-day New Rochelle, New York.

In 1643, Hutchinson and five of her children were killed in a battle with Native Americans. Her eight-year-old daughter was carried away and remained with the tribe for four years. By then she had forgotten her own language and all her friends. Much to her dismay, she was returned to the Dutch when the parties finally made peace.

The establishment of small groups of rival Christians, however, was not the Puritan's real problem. Even before King's Chapel was envisioned, the children of the original settlers began to slip from the religious zeal of their parents. Many could not meet the standards for church membership their parents had set and they failed to show they had been truly converted. Membership began to decline and in order to check that decline, in 1662 church leaders proposed what was called the Half-Way Covenant.

From the beginning, the children of full church members had been baptized as babies and hence were considered church members. However, until and unless they met the full requirements of adult membership they could not take communion. The 1662 Half-Way Covenant allowed such unconfirmed members to also present their children for baptism, though these children could not take communion until and unless they also later met the full requirements. The move allowed participation in the church by more people, but the declining number allowed to take communion became a public sign of the decline in spirituality among those members.

The Salem Witch Trials

While trying to find ways to encourage church members' spiritual life and fending off the efforts of rival churches, the Puritans discovered still another serious problem. Several adolescent girls, including the daughter and the niece of the minister of Salem Village (today the town of Danvers, Massachusetts) had been entertaining themselves by predicting the future using a folk magic technique—staring into an egg white. Their activities were discovered by their parents in 1692 when they began to have convulsions. Forced to explain their actions, they complained that the family maid had bewitched them. Their initial accusation prompted an investigation—witchcraft being a serious matter in the Puritan community—and within a short time others were being named.

Accepting the word of the girls, who named additional witches while in their convulsive state, the courts added testimony of residents against neighbors who, for example, told stories of misfortunes coming to them after someone had cursed them. There had been previous trials for witchcraft in the Puritan colonies, but the situation in Salem Village quickly worsened. Within a few weeks the jails were filled with all those accused, and within months some 20 people were executed, most by hanging. Only after 20 people had died and leading citizens were affected by these accusations were the trials brought to an end.

Finally the court began to listen to the warnings of people such as prominent Boston minister Cotton Mather (1663–1728) against convicting people based on unsupported statements by the girls. Mather, who initially supported the investigations, ultimately had to personally intervene with the governor to end the trials. As the members of the community realized what they had done, they formally repented their actions, and the trial ultimately helped discredit belief in witchcraft.

Lutherans in Young America

While British Anglicans and Congregationalists were the distinct majority in the colonial Protestant community, they were not alone. The first Lutherans to arrive and form a congregation were part of the brief attempt of Sweden to colonize North America. The Swedish settlers occupied a small parcel of land along the Delaware River in 1638 and their first minister, Reorus Torkillus (d.1643), arrived the next year. The Swedes surrendered control of their colony to the Dutch in 1655, but Lutheran worship was allowed to continue.

Meanwhile, a few Dutch Lutherans were among those who settled along the Hudson River up stream from New Amsterdam. The first mention of their presence was in 1643, when it was noted that they were among those that the colony did not permit to have worship services. Six years later, however, the community had grown enough that it could petition Lutherans in Holland for a pastor. The owners of the Dutch East India Company (the Dutch settlement being, like the other colonies, an economic adventure) had no problems with the request, but the Dutch Reformed ministers were incensed. The request was debated for five years and finally denied. The Lutheran minister who had arrived in the meantime was not allowed to work. He eventually returned to Europe and the Dutch Lutherans had to await the arrival of the British in 1664 before they were allowed to organize.

Lutheranism remained but a small force in colonial America until the 1720s, when a large number of Germans (more than 60,000) began the move to Pennsylvania, many becoming indentured servants to pay their passage. Congregations were opened in German Town (1728) and Philadelphia (1730). Finally, in 1742, the minister most responsible for creating an American Lutheran church, Henry Muhlenberg (1711–1787), arrived. Muhlenberg spoke four languages, was personable, and a capable organizer. Six years after his arrival he led in the formation of the Ministerium of Pennsylvania, a Lutheran Synod (an association of congregations and ministers). He served until his death in 1787 and left three sons in the clergy to carry on. One who would serve as a general in the revolutionary army and one later as speaker of the U. S. House of Representatives.

The Reformed Church

The Reformed Church in America points proudly to its Marble Collegiate congregation as the oldest continuously existing congregation in America. The Collegiate Reformed Protestant Dutch Church of New York City was organized in 1628 when Peter Minuit (1580–1638), who was famous for supposedly purchasing Manhattan for $24, was governor of New Amsterdam. It has held worship services for more that 370 years. Granted a royal charter by the British crown in 1696, the church is also the oldest corporation in the United States.

As the Dutch expanded northward through the Hudson Valley, additional Reformed congregations were founded. Some of these were the product of the patroon system. Any man who brought 50 or more colonists to New Netherlands would be named a patroon, provided free transportation across the Atlantic, and granted a large tract of land to farm. Among his obligations, each patroon was supposed to support a minister of the Reformed church. The Van Rensselaer patroonship, near the present site of Albany, New York, was the first and most successful, and the site of the second Reformed Church in the colonies.

The expansion of New Netherlands set the stage for the arrival of one of the more infamous characters in American history, Peter Stuyvesant (c.1592–1672), the director general of the Dutch East India Company, who arrived in New Amsterdam in 1647. Signs of things to come were seen in his very first act—a new law that restricted the sale of alcohol and instituted strict observance of the Sabbath (on Sunday). Among other things, the law prohibited the consumption of liquor during worship services. The next year he ordered a second Sunday afternoon preaching service and demanded all attend.

His zealousness in promoting the Reformed Church led to his denying all others the right to form congregations. Prancing around

Not quite a fair trade
Stepping ashore from Holland, Peter Minuit offered what amounted to trinkets to Native Americans in exchange for what became Manhattan Island.

with the peg leg he got when he lost a leg in battle in the Caribbean, he ruled as an autocrat, except for those few times he was overruled by company bosses in Holland on such matters as the acceptance of the first Jews to settle in the colonies. Ultimately, he would be forced to surrender the colony to the British, but not before the Reformed Church was an established, growing entity.

The Presbyterians

Of the Protestant churches, the Presbyterians were the last to arrive. Presbyterians (Puritans who favored the leadership of the church by presbyters, or elders) took control of the established church in Scotland and were the dominant Puritan faction through the 17th century in England. Those few who moved to America in the 17th century tended to be absorbed by the Congregationalists in New England. It wasn't until 1684 that the Rev. Francis Makemie (1638–1708) founded the first Presbyterian congregation at Snow Hill, Maryland. He encouraged the formation of additional congregations throughout the colonies, and in

1706 led in the formation of the first presbytery, based in Philadelphia. The next year, running into the same problems other groups faced with intolerant colonial authorities, he was arrested. Though acquitted, he was forced to pay the costs for his trial and imprisonment.

The first Presbyterian synod (forerunner of the General Assembly) was formed in 1717. In the 1720s it passed what was termed the Adopting Act, requiring assent to the Westminster Confession of Faith by all members of the synod and by all candidates for admission to the presbytery.

Presbyterianism in the colonies came from three sources. First, Congregationalists who moved from New England to other colonies showed a marked tendency to turn Presbyterian, which required no change in basic doctrine. Second, during the 17th century, England made a great effort to populate northern Ireland with transplanted Scots. By the end of the century, each time a problem arose in northern Ireland, many Irish left for North America rather than returning to their original home. Finally, many Scotsmen came directly to

Stuyvesant and the Jews of New Amsterdam

In 1654, the Brazilian city of Recife, which had been a Dutch possession, came under Portuguese rule. The Jewish people living there feared persecution (discrimination because of their religion), and many Jewish families decided to leave. One small group convinced the French captain of a ship called the *Saint Catherine* to take them to the Dutch colony of New Amsterdam, and promised that their relatives would send the money for the voyage when they arrived.

After six months at sea, 23 Jews arrived in New Amsterdam. The captain of the Saint Catherine immediately went to court, claiming that the Jews had not paid him for their voyage. Some were sent to jail and others were forced to sell off all their belongings to pay the debt.

New Amsterdam governor Peter Stuyvesant heard about the Jews on the Saint Catherine and immediately wrote to his employers at the Dutch West India Company, stating his intention to send them away. But the Jews also wrote to the Dutch West India Company. They reminded the directors of the company that they were loyal Dutch citizens. In addition, many of the directors were themselves Jews. They told Stuyvesant that the Jews could stay in New Amsterdam.

After receiving this unexpected reply, Stuyvesant let the Jewish settlers stay, but made life difficult for them. He prevented them from building a synagogue and from standing as guards for the settlement.

Preacher man
George Whitefield's powerful and uplifting sermons and speeches gave rise to the Great Awakening, a spiritual revival the colonies underwent in the years before the American Revolution. This woodcut was created in the late 19th century by Nathaniel Hone.

America. The Scots and Scotch-Irish spread throughout British America. In the wake of their arrival the Presbyterian church grew at a remarkable pace. It attained a foremost position in New York, Pennsylvania, and New Jersey.

The Great Awakening

By the 1740s, the European Protestants had become the dominant religious force in the British colonies along the Atlantic. However, they were split along ideological grounds, especially related to the mode of church governance—leadership by bishops (Anglican), by congregations (New England Congregationalists), or by elders (Presbyterians and Reformed). Membership was spread among the 13 colonies from Georgia to Maine. Thus Protestants were divided by loyalties to their own colony as well as to their own denomination.

Further, while growing at a respectable rate, the Christian community remained only a small minority in the colonies and its ministers were constantly bemoaning the immorality and lack of religion they saw running rampant among their potential flocks. Into this time stepped a remarkable man who would have a profound effect on the shape of American religion.

George Whitefield (1714–1770) was a Church of England minister who had associated with John Wesley, the founder of Methodism, while a fellow student at Oxford University. With the same drive that raised Methodism to prominence in England, Whitefield added a broad ecumenical spirit and a passion for lost souls. He also had what were possibly the best oratorical skills of the century. He made his first rather limited preaching tour in the colonies in 1739, but returned in 1740 for an extensive tour of the colonies that took him from Savannah, Georgia, to York, Maine, with important stops in Philadelphia, Boston, and Northampton, Massachusetts, where he met the Rev. Jonathan Edwards (1703–1758).

Several times a week, dressed in white wig and black robe, he addressed crowds in the thousands. His words resonated with common people, leaving them pondering the condition of their souls. He even moved the skeptical Benjamin Franklin, who listened as Whitefield addressed some 20,000 people in Philadelphia without the aid of any sound amplification equipment. Though doctrinally sound, he spoke to peoples' hearts more than their minds. He won support in every denomination and likewise provoked critics of his willingness to avoid those subjects that divided people. Among those attracted to the "revival" of spirituality that Whitefield envisioned was Jonathan Edwards, later recognized as the greatest American theological mind of his generation, who promoted the revival throughout New England.

While Whitefield aimed his efforts at the spiritual regeneration of his listeners, his tours through the colonies had another unexpected consequence. He came to the colonies as a Protestant Christian evangelist, not the representative of the Church of England. He became a celebrity and his preaching services a mass event anticipated by members of all churches and no church. Whitefield was "happening" and his sermons transformed individuals in all denominations. He took his revival to all of the colonies, and the Great Awakening he provoked was also the first event shared by all the colonies—a significant event in the rising self-consciousness of the British colonies as one entity. Increasingly after Whitefield's first tours, other ministers also went on tour throughout the colonies on behalf of God and His salvation.

ECUMENICAL

Ecumenical means belonging to or accepted by the Christian church throughout the world, regardless of denomination.

2

The Protestant Church in a New Land

ONE OF THE LESSER-KNOWN EVENTS LEADING TO THE AMERICAN Revolution began with the failure of the tobacco crop in Virginia in 1755. At the time, Anglican clergy were paid by the government with tobacco. Having no tobacco, the legislature voted simply to pay the ministers in cash—two pence for each pound of tobacco. On hearing the news, the clergy protested. The going rate for tobacco was twice as high. The legislature had, in effect, cut their salary in half. Then, the King's Privy Council in England came to the ministers' rescue and removed that law. Based on the ruling, the ministers sued for back pay, and they might have won had not a young lawyer by the name of Patrick Henry stepped in. Henry argued that in striking down the Virginia law, the king had broken the implied contract between the governed (that is, the citizens of Virginia) and the ruler, thereby forfeiting "all rights to his subject's obedience." Henry's arguments in favor of Virginia making its own laws prevailed, and the ministers failed to get their back pay. The Anglican ministers fell victim to one of the first vocal shots of the coming war.

Religion and Independence

The so called Virginia "Parson's Cause," however, was a relatively minor issue as the prospect of real shooting approached. All of the clergy throughout the

37

colonies, especially those who were sympathetic to the colonists' demands, had first to answer what for them was a life-or-death question: Did the colonists' demands constitute sufficient grounds to take up arms against a duly established government? Some, like the Anglicans, were closely identified with the British government, although they received their salary from the rebellious colonial authorities. Those in New England had spent years in legal maneuvering to keep their bishopless church system, and they often saw British authorities as another obstacle to be overcome. However, playing legal games was one thing and openly defying established authority was quite another.

The crux of the problem rested on the common reading of the Apostle Paul's seemingly straightforward statement to believers in ancient Rome. Paul wrote, "Let every soul be subject to the higher powers (government). For there is no power but of God; the powers that be are ordained of God. Whosoever therefore resists the power, resists the ordinance of God; and they that resist shall receive to themselves damnation. For rulers are not a terror to good works, but to the evil" (Romans 13: 1-3). Because of this, revolting against government was a serious theological issue. Most of the clergy had to be convinced, and on the eve of the war, many were not.

It is estimated that half a million to a million residents, between 20 and 40 percent of the population (apart from the slaves), were opposed to independence. Loyalists emerged in every colony, though they were most numerous in the Mid-Atlantic and Southern colonies. Of the churches, the Episcopalians were most identified with the loyalist cause; the Presbyterians and Congregationalists most with the patriots.

The most prominent minister aligned early on with the Revolution was probably the Presbyterian John Witherspoon (1723–1794). He represented New Jersey in the Continental Congress for six years (1776–1782), during which time he added his name to the Declaration of Independence and served on more than 100 committees. He had moved from England to serve as president of Princeton College, and as the war began, critics accused him of subverting the purposes of the school as he pushed its students and faculty to back independence.

Rather than actually bearing arms as Muhlenberg did (see the box opposite), many of his colleagues, such as New Jersey Presbyterian James Caldwell (1734-1781), served as chaplains during the War. Caldwell is remembered for his actions at a battle at Springfield, New Jersey, on

A Preacher Goes to War

Rev. Peter Muhlenberg (1746–1807) of Woodstock, Virginia, the eldest son of pioneer Lutheran organizer Henry Muhlenberg, is remembered for his bold stand for independence. On Sunday morning, January 21, 1776, as the story goes, he chose to preach from Ecclesiastes 3:1-8. As he reached his discussion of verse eight, and the phrase, [there is] "a time for peace and a time for war," he removed the robe in which he normally preached to show the congregation the uniform of a Virginia militia officer underneath. He declared, "And this is a time for war." He then invited any man who could to join the company he was raising. Three hundred responded and left town with him to constitute the core of what became known as the Muhlenberg Brigade.

The parson rose to the rank of major general during the war, his military career climaxing at Yorktown, the final major battle of the war. Criticized by his brother Frederick (also a minister) for actually bearing arms, Muhlenberg responded, as quoted in James' Adams book *Yankee Doodle Went to Church*, "I am a clergyman, it is true, but I am a member of society as well as the poorest layman, and my liberty is as dear to me as any man. Shall I then sit still, and enjoy myself at home, when the best blood of the continent is spilling? Heaven forbid it!"

June 23, 1780. The troops he served with ran out of wadding for their muskets. Caldwell was reported to have gone into a nearby Presbyterian church, from which he took a stack of hymnals written by a Dr. Watts. He distributed them to the soldiers, telling them to "put Watts into them, boys."

From the perspective of 200 years later, we can understand the difficult choice faced by religious people in 1776 when asked to support a revolution, even though it was a popular one. As one Anglican layman and colonial legislator, Isaac Wilkins, put it when he returned to England in 1775, "It has been my constant maxim through life to do my duty conscientiously and to trust the issue of my actions to the Almighty. . . I leave America and ever endearing connection because I will not raise my hand against my Sovereign, nor will I draw my sword against my Country," (as quoted in Erdman's *Handbook of Christianity*, published in 1983).

Still more conflicted were the Quakers and members of the other small sects of the radical Reformation, such as the German Mennonites. They held positions of prominence in Philadelphia and elsewhere, but were dedicated pacifists. They still remembered when, quite apart from their pacifism or plain dress, just being a Quaker was enough to face scorn, persecution, and even death. But in 1776, the Philadelphia Yearly Meeting stood firm; they not only opposed members going to

A meeting of Friends
This 1880 woodcut from a Swedish book about North America shows a Philadelphia prayer meeting of the Society of Friends, also known as the Quakers. Both women and men wore distinctive headgear and dark, plain clothing.

war but added, "It is our judgment that such who make religious profession with us, and do either openly or by connivance, pay any fine, penalty, or tax, in lieu of their personal services for carrying on war, or who do consent to, and allow their children, apprentices, or servants to act therein do thereby violate our Christian testimony, and by so doing manifest that they are not in religious fellowship with us."

As the war progressed, however, the majority of the ministers and laity came to agree with New England Presbyterian minister Abraham Keteltas (1732–1798), who could not have put it any more clearly in 1777 (as quoted in the 1998 book *Re-forming the Center: American Protestantism 1900 to the Present*): "The most precious remains of civil liberty the world can now boast of, are lodged in our hands. . . [This war] is the cause of truth, against error and falsehood. . . the cause of pure and undefiled religion, against bigotry, superstition, and human inventions. . . . In short it is the cause of heaven against hell, of the kind parent of the universe against the prince of darkness and the destroyer of the human race."

The war lasted for seven years. The patriots finally won, but the war cost the Protestant churches dearly. Few new ministers had emerged during the war, and many had either left the soon-to-be-independent country or had been killed in the fighting. Most noted that the climate of war had driven many people from religion, and the patriot cause had placed a number of people of very liberal religious leaning in power. People such as Thomas Jefferson and Benjamin Franklin were what were known as Deists. While they believed in God and the moral order, they were skeptical of traditional Christianity, the concept of salvation, and the supernatural relationship with the Divine it inferred. While more orthodox voices like that of Witherspoon were certainly present in the new government's deliberations, the ideas of Jefferson and his colleague James Madison dominated.

Life After the Revolution

The most important action relative to the churches in the new nation was the adoption of the First Amendment to the United States Constitution. In melding the original 13 independent-minded colonies into a united nation, the founding fathers had to remove all of the factors that would keep them apart. One such factor was choosing a national church. The Anglicans were most numerous, but the Congregationalists controlled New England. Unable to decide between them, the members of Congress solved the problem by letting each state make its own decision. Congress decided against having a national church—a bold move in the 1780s. In its place, they created a purely non-religious government that would allow no denomination first place and that would protect the rights of all churches to exist. States could (as did Massachusetts with the Congregational or Puritan Church) designate an established church; however, most states could not muster the support for such an official church, and soon even Massachusetts gave up on the idea.

In resolving the religion question, Jefferson and his colleagues turned their problem into a national virtue. As they saw it, the tyranny of clerical rule (which many had experienced) was to be replaced with religious liberty and the peoples' freedom from government in their religious life. In the First Amendment, the federal government agreed that, "Congress shall make no law respecting an establishment of religion, or prohibiting the free exercise thereof . . . ." In 1801, Jefferson explained his understanding of this First Amendment in a famous letter written to the Danbury (Connecticut) Baptist Association, in which he suggested that the amendment erected a "wall of separation" between the church and state. His approach to the separate role of religion and government would come to dominate later interpretations of the First Amendment, and would enter into official documents through rulings of the United States Supreme Court.

The First Amendment quickly and completely reorganized American religious life, at least for most people. As states adopted clauses similar to the First Amendment into their constitutions, many familiar religious structures passed into oblivion. Churches would no longer received state funds and ministers were no longer given their salary out of the public treasury. Such curtailing of state support had little effect on the Baptists and Methodists, but caused significant change in those larger Protestant churches, especially the Anglican and Congregational churches, that had formerly enjoyed some state support. They had to rethink their existence as just one denomination among others.

Denied government funds, the churches had to turn to their members for direct support if they were to survive. Although suffering the most from loss of state funds, the Anglicans and Congregationalists discovered that they had an important resource: They served the majority of the wealthier and more powerful people in the new nation. Those citizens most able to support them were already among their adherents. And under the new voluntary system, wealthy laypeople proved, in many cases, to be generous patrons of their church.

Church Life Changes

This new system of religious support necessitated some dramatic alterations of church life. Now churches had to plan around free will offerings that could radically vary from year to year and month to month (especially in farming regions). They had to retrain laypeople who had been freed of religious taxes to instead give to their parish. Without the backing of the state for their religious cause, ministers could not simply demand behavioral conformity; they had to learn to cajole and persuade their listeners to live up to Christian ideals.

Churches also had to reorganize to accommodate their new way of life. For most of the churches, reorganization continued a natural process of growth and development. Thus the General Assembly of the Presbyterian Church was organized in 1789.

As Lutherans expanded into different parts of the country they created additional synods to serve new constituencies. Congregationalists had little trouble continuing their local associations of churches. The Reformed Church, which had already taken a step to organize independently of its Dutch parent, created a fully autonomous Reformed Church in America in 1792. However, the Anglicans faced the greatest obstacle to adjusting to the new situation.

Anglicans After the War

For sure, there were Anglicans who had supported the Revolution. When Paul Revere made his famous ride to warn the patriots at Lexington and Concord of the approaching British Army, he was signaled from the tower of Christ Church. The pre-Revolutionary assistant rector of Trinity Church in New York City was forced out of his parish and wound up spending part of the war in a patriot uniform. However, Anglicans sympathetic to independence immediately ran into a problem with their Prayer Book, the book that included the liturgy used in Anglican worship: It contained a prayer for the king of England. Even as initial hostilities broke out, there were calls to edit the text and in May of 1776, the Maryland legislature (where the Church of England was still the established church) voted to delete the royal prayer.

But in spite of the several patriots, most of the Anglican ministers were loyal to the land of their birth, and as the war progressed, they abandoned their parishes for England or Canada. After the war, the church was short of ministers, responsible for a large number of parishioners, and without a bishop to provide leadership. The remaining ministers met to begin rebuilding. They removed any remaining references to the crown and the Church of England from the Prayer Book, at the same time requesting Church officials in England to consecrate one or more bishops from among the American clergy. However, there was a critical obstacle. According to British law, before anyone could be consecrated, that person had to pledge their loyalty to the British crown. It took several years to resolve the issue, but finally in 1787, William White (1747–1830) and Samuel Provoost (1742–1815, the former assistant rector from New York) were consecrated.

Both bishops had outstanding careers, but White became the dominant force in the church. The son of wealthy parents, he emerged very early as a supporter of the Revolution, and beginning in 1777, he

NO MORE KINGS

On May 25, 1776, the Maryland government decreed that "every Prayer and Petition for the King's Majesty, in the book of Common Prayer [used in all Anglican churches] . . . be henceforth omitted in all Churches and Chapels in this Province." The offending passage stated the worshipper's desire that God "keep and strengthen in the true worshipping of thee, in righteousness and holiness of life, thy servant GEORGE, our most gracious King and Governour." It was replaced with a request that "it might please thee [God] to bless the honorable Congress with Wisdom to discern and Integrity to pursue the true Interest of the United States."

When the Senate first convened in New York City on April 6, 1789, one of its first orders of business was to appoint a committee to recommend a candidate for chaplain. On April 25, the Senate elected the Right Reverend Samuel Provoost, Episcopal Bishop of New York, as its first chaplain.

Since that time, the Senate has been served by chaplains of various religious denominations, including Episcopalians (19), Methodists (17), Presbyterians (14), Baptists (6), Unitarians (2), Congregationalists (1), Lutherans (1), and Roman Catholics (1). The Senate has also appointed guest chaplains representative of all the world's major religious faiths.

In addition to opening the Senate each day with a prayer, the current Senate chaplain's duties include spiritual care and counseling for senators, their families, and their staffs—a combined constituency of more than 6,000 people.

served as the chaplain of the Continental Congress, until the federal government moved from Philadelphia to New York in 1789. His colleague, Bishop Provoost of New York, became the first chaplain to the U.S. Senate. White knew most of the founding fathers, and while lacking memorable oratorical skills, was an outstanding conversationalist and negotiator. He led the Episcopal Church (as the independent American Anglicans came to be known) to adopt a more democratic structure. He remained active into his 80s, and is largely responsible for the Anglicans finding a place in the post-Revolutionary United States.

With White at the helm, the Episcopalians were able to quickly shed their loyalist image and emerge as the church of America's elite. During the next two centuries, the Episcopal Church would nurture more of America's political and business leaders than any other church. St. John's Church, located across the street from the White House, became known as the church of the presidents, as all presidents since James Madison have worshiped there, some quite regularly.

With a new government in place, the new nation was ready to move forward, and by the 1790s, the Protestant churches were quite prepared to move forward with it. While the Methodists and Baptists were seizing the opportunity on the frontier to win the pioneering masses, and would soon surpass the older churches in membership, the older Protestant churches offered the United States their assets in social and intellectual leadership. Though not necessarily the largest religious bodies, they possessed the tools to give moral and spiritual direction to the culture and would dominate the religious life of the nation well into the 20th century.

Early Protestant Educational Endeavors

The Puritans landed in New England in 1620, and a mere 16 years later they established Harvard College in a town across the river named for the school so many of the clergy had attended, Cambridge. The college itself was named for John Harvard, a young minister who passed away in 1638 and bequeathed to the new school his large library and half his estate. The school was not officially attached to the Congregationalist churches, but none doubted the reason for its founding—training future ministers. An early brochure describing the school suggested that the major motive in its founding was the dread of "an illiterate Ministry to the Churches." Its curriculum steadily expanded to include all

On the Harvard Yard
Congregationalist minister John Harvard gave the land the Puritans needed to found a new college. Today his statue overlooks the main yard of Harvard, one of the world's most distinguished universities.

the arts and sciences and many professional specialties. As Harvard grew, many suggested that it was moving away from its initial purpose. Thus in 1701, the Congregationalists in Connecticut founded a second school, Yale University, more committed to Christian purposes.

The founding of Harvard and Yale clearly demonstrated the European Protestant commitment to education, appropriate for a movement that had been founded at a university in Germany. Yale, especially, came to serve a broad range of churches, and many future Presbyterian and Anglican ministers were trained there during the colonial period. Anglicans in Virginia moved to establish a college through the colonial legislatures, and in 1693 succeeded in opening the College of William and Mary after Rev. James Blair secured a royal charter and the support of the Archbishop of Canterbury (the head of the Church of England). The Archbishop's successors remained William and Mary's designated chancellors until 1762.

Through the 1720s, Presbyterians almost totally relied on Yale for educating their ministers, but at the end of the decade the church was caught up in a debate over whether ministers had to consent to the Westminster Confession of Faith, the traditional British Presbyterian statement of their belief. It was not that Presbyterians disagreed so much about what the Confession taught, but some rejected the church giving allegiance to what they saw as a man-made document.

As this controversy continued, a young Irish minister, William Tennant (1673–1746), began a school at Neshaminy, Pennsylvania, to train ministers. He placed less emphasis on the Confession and more on a heart-felt religious life that he termed "experimental orthodoxy." Beginning with four students, in 1735 he built a log cabin that came to be known as the Log College. The more conservative group in the church moved to counter the influence of the Log College by requiring its graduates to submit to an examination before being accepted as ministers.

The Log College declined in the mid 1740s, and the desire of the Presbyterians to have a college of their own prompted the formation of the College of New Jersey. It moved into facilities in Princeton, New Jersey, in 1756. The new college attracted students from throughout the colonies, all of whom came under the influence of its long-term president, John Witherspoon. Given Witherspoon's support of the Revolution, it was not surprising to find that a high percentage of the delegates who wrote the American Constitution were Princeton graduates.

Meanwhile, the Dutch-speaking Reformed Church struggled to Americanize and founded a school to train ministers in America rather than send candidates to Holland. First, in 1766 the Reformed ministers opened Queen's College at New Brunswick, New Jersey. Then, after the American Revolution, they founded a second school, a theological seminary, in Brooklyn, New York. In 1810 this seminary moved to New Brunswick and merged into Queen's College as its program in theological education. Queen's College evolved into the present day Rutgers University.

Protestants and Theology

The older Protestant churches are also distinguished from the newer, evangelical churches by their attention to theology, which is the systematic study of the relationship of God and the world He created. Theology has been an ongoing concern of all of the Christian churches from the time of the ancient church. By the second century, theologians emerged to make intellectual sense of biblical writings and documents and explain the faith to the learned Pagans in whose world the church was growing.

Over the years, different branches of the church have given varying attention to the study of theology, but Protestants were noteworthy for the value they placed on intellectual attainments and the accomplishments of their educated elite. Luther, a theologian by trade, wrote numerous theological treatises, and Calvin put his legal training to work in creating the first systematic Protestant theology text. The majority of the clergymen who brought Protestantism to America were trained at a university and committed themselves to perpetuating their educational attainments among the next generations of ministers.

The American frontier did not yield a great deal of time for the kind of quiet reflection generally considered necessary for theological thought. However, by the beginning of the 1700s, Congregationalist ministers in Boston were turning out theological texts, possibly the most noteworthy being Cotton Mather's *Magnalia Christi Americana* (1703) in which he reflected on what he saw as God's particular dealing with the Puritan community. Mather wrote that he believed that the "Christian religion, flying from the deprivations of Europe to the American Strand," was especially blessed by God. He wrote that God had shone his light for Christians on an "Indian Wilderness."

Another Congregationalist minister, Jonathan Edwards (1703–1758), became America's first great theologian. A precocious child, he mastered several languages by the age of 13, when he entered Yale. Later, as pastor of the church at Northampton, Massachusetts, he observed firsthand the revivals of the Great Awakening of the 1730s and 1740s (see page 34), including the unusual behavior that accompanied them. In a church noted for its decorum, people cried out and shouted, their bodies convulsed, and some fell on the floor as if dead. It was to Edwards' credit that he did not simply dismiss what was occurring, as many of his colleagues did. Seeing the good that came from the revivals, he tried to understand them. What he saw became the basis of many of his later writings.

Toward the end of his life, in *History of Redemption* (1776), Edwards laid out the story of God's work of redemption from the fall of humanity into sin, to the saving work of Christ, to the life of the church. Human history was moving toward the kingdom of God, he wrote. The revivals he had witnessed as a young man were a forerunner of the coming Golden Age. History was propelled forward by these occasional seasons of revival and spiritual awakening, carried out by "remarkable outpourings of the Spirit."

PAGANS

Pagans (the word literally means "country dwellers") believed in many gods, as in the ancient Roman and Greek religions. This contrasts with the monotheism of Christianity, Judaism, and Islam. Monotheists believe in one God, and often use "Pagan" as a derogatory term.

Influential thinker
Jonathan Edwards was the most prominent theologian of the colonial period. His work in helping to define the American way of practicing Protestantism has had long-lasting impact.

Science and Theology

By the end of the 19th century, Christian theologians were reacting to new discoveries in science and changes in the makeup of America, especially the growth of urban centers, which were being swelled with an increasing flow of immigrants. New scientific findings, especially the work of Charles Darwin, challenged some traditional Christian assumptions. For example, Darwin suggested that over many thousands of years, the animal kingdom had evolved from lesser to more complex forms culminating in the emergence of the human species. At the same time, geologists were describing an earth that was far older than the 6,000 to 10,000 years that many believed was described in the opening chapters of the Bible.

The conflict between a traditional Christian understanding of history based upon a literal reading of Genesis, the first book of the Bible, caused many to view science as attacking the Bible and undermining its authority. They developed arguments to defend traditional, literal readings of the Bible and maintain its role at the center of Protestantism. One of the more heralded efforts in this regard was carried out by a group of thinkers at Princeton University. They argued for the literal truth of the biblical text, which they asserted was infallible (true when talking about faith and morals) and inerrant (true when discussing matters of scientific or historical fact). Their approach laid the foundation for a popular movement to defend the essentials of traditional Protestantism in the early 20th century, called Fundamentalism.

The exponents of the Princeton theology were opposed by other theologians who found the arguments of Darwin and other scientists persuasive and who tried to understand the biblical text in the context of ongoing scientific findings. Some, for example, argued that evolution was merely the means by which God accomplished His creative will. Such views came to dominate the teachings of the larger churches and their schools where ministers were trained.

The increasing prominence of the new sciences in the academic world created a new theology that responded to the world being described by physicists, biologists, geologists, and psychologists. Scientists regularly publish new findings that alter our view of the cosmos and human society. Theology has had to redefine itself in conversation with scientists and the ongoing understanding of the meaning of their latest discoveries about the world and the universe. The process of adapting the Christian tradition to an ever-changing world continues to be a major task of the churches' contemporary leaders.

How to Spread the Word

At the same time, Protestants also argued about how they were to proceed with the work of evangelizing the world. Through the 19th century, the churches had grown significantly by their evangelistic efforts, especially revival meetings at which attendees were invited to accept a personal relationship to God and Jesus Christ and join the church.

However, in the emerging urban complexes, many felt that revivalism was not appropriate. Here, the churches developed a different approach. They concentrated on efforts to reorder society in a more Christian way, as a just society that cared for everyone's needs. Such leaders as Walter Rauschenbusch and Washington Gladden believed that God's kingdom could be built (and people would respond to the Christian message) if a more Christian world was organized. In following this new way, they directed the church's attention to Jesus' primary message announcing the coming kingdom of God. Their approach came to be known as the Social Gospel. Fundamentalism and the

Social Gospel vied for the attention of the larger Protestant churches through the early 20th century.

Protestants Merge Together

The older Protestant churches, now joined by the newer evangelical churches (such as Methodists, Baptists, and Disciples of Christ), began the 20th century as the largest religious community in America. However, it was a community divided among a growing number of denominations. The Protestant community was also challenged by a variety of cultural changes brought on by scientific discoveries, the increasingly diverse culture created by immigrants from around the world, and a new self-consciousness about culture and society coming forth from sociologists and psychologists. Early in the 20th century two massive contradictory trends became apparent.

First, as the new century began, Protestants attempted to unify the structures of their many denominations. One sign of that unity would be the formation of the Federal Council of Churches (FCC) in 1908. Most of the larger Protestant bodies joined the FCC in the hope that it could supply Protestants with a common voice. They also hoped it would become the instrument for reducing competition between denominations. Additionally, they saw the FCC as helping them all in common action against various social problems, such as poverty, child labor, aging, and war. The attention to social issues was embodied in the Social Creed of the Churches (see the box at left), adopted by the FCC at the time of its formation.

Cooperation through the council (which was renamed the National Council of Churches of Christ in the U.S.A. [NCCC] in 1950) also led a number of churches to consider the possibility of merging their organizations. One of the earlier notable mergers occurred in 1906 when the Presbyterian Church in the U.S.A. united with the Cumberland Presbyterian Church.

Possibly the most significant mergers, however, were to occur within the Lutheran family of churches. Throughout the 19th century immigrants from predominantly Lutheran European countries such as Germany and Sweden settled across the United States. In most cases, regional synods (groups of related congregations) based on language and national heritage were founded. In the decades after the Civil War, Lutherans of the same national/linguistic heritage began to form na-

tional bodies. Then through the 20th century, especially spurred by the general cultural pressure to drop languages other than English during World War I, Lutherans began to associate across their ethnic boundaries. The result was a series of mergers, the most important of which led to the formation of the American Lutheran Church (1960) and the Lutheran Church in America (1962). These two bodies, along with the smaller Association of Evangelical Lutheran Churches, merged in 1988 to form the Evangelical Lutheran Church in America.

Meanwhile, Presbyterians had completed their steps to reunite nationally in 1983 with the formation of the Presbyterian Church (U.S.A.).

Conservatives vs. Liberals

Not all members were happy with the more liberal ideas that were becoming the dominant trends in the larger Protestant churches. By the end of the 19th century, more conservative church leaders protested the new theological perspectives being proposed by liberal theologians. They suggested that the Social Gospel took energy away from the church's evangelistic task; that acceptance of Darwin's ideas about evolution contradicted biblical truth; and that geological findings contradicted traditional understandings of creation.

The conservative backlash showed itself in a series of challenges to the ministerial credentials of liberal ministers and the jobs of liberal professors of religion at church schools. A variety of heresy

Protestants and the Social Gospel

The emphasis on social concerns within the larger Protestant bodies found expression in a major new theological movement, usually termed the Social Gospel. Theologians such as Walter Rauschenbusch (1861–1918) suggested that the primary message of Jesus was the announcement of the coming kingdom of God. That being the case, the churches, he reasoned, should engage the social order and attempt to create a more just social system. For those who believed in the Social Gospel, justice was seen as the social embodiment of love.

The Social Gospel led many Protestants to consider socialism as offering a more equitable economic system for the country than capitalism, and others affirmed a belief in pacifism as a route to end war.

The emphasis on the Social Gospel and its desire to build a more just social order was often contrasted to an earlier focus on each individual's salvation. Social gospel advocates observed Christian society evolving into the kingdom of God on earth and people coming to Christ through their participation in that more just and equal society. This view added energy to traditional Protestant views that God's reign would eventually be established on earth.

CAPITALISM An economic system in which private or corporate ownership makes the basic decisions about distribution of goods and wealth, usually based on competition in a free market.

SOCIALISM An economic system in which the basic means of production are owned collectively and in which all members of a society, regardless of their level of input into creating the wealth, share in the fruits of what is produced.

---

trials, with mixed results, were held between 1890 and the beginning of World War I (1914). Then, beginning in the 1920s, Protestant churches faced challenges at their national meetings to the new directions being taken by different pastors, church administrators, and seminary professors. The result was a number of angry confrontations during which control of the denominations passed, in most cases, to the more liberal wings of the churches.

In light of their loss of influence within the larger Protestant bodies, many conservative leaders left their old churches. Thus, as many Protestants were responding to the call for greater unity, the trend toward cooperation was countered by the establishment of many new Protestant denominations. Often, the merger of two church bodies would become the occasion of more conservative members withdrawing and setting up one or more new denominations. (A few of the older Protestant churches, such as the Lutheran Church-Missouri Synod and the Christian Reformed Church did not participate in this liberalizing trend.)

Through the 20th century the newer conservative denominations and the remaining conservative members in the liberal Protestant churches reacted to what they saw as the ongoing drift of the liberal churches away from Protestant tradition. The ongoing debates within larger denominations and even within local congregations will probably color most issues in the Protestant world in the near future.

Changes in the Churches

In the last half of the 20th century, churches were also disturbed by revisions in modes of worship, some instituted in parishes by innovative pastors, some initiated at the national level. Possibly the most controversial changes in the church came with the widespread acceptance of women into the ordained ministry. While some churches had ordained women earlier, Protestant denominations in the 1970s began to actively promote women's equality, recruit women as seminary students, and work with congregations toward hiring female pastors. The Episcopal Church felt this change more than most churches, and its acceptance of female priests in the mid-1970s led to a significant minority leaving and establishing rival Anglican denominations.

In addition, as the 21st century begins, the issues of abortion and homosexuality dominate debates within the Protestant churches. All three of these issues are discussed in detail in chapter 4.

Today, Protestant churches find themselves in an ongoing tension of their own making. On the one hand, they seek to be true to the Christian tradition. Generation by generation, they reaffirm that tradition. At the same time, they insist that it is not an unchanging tradition, that it is in constant need of reformation and development. They point to earlier changes in the churches' attitude toward slavery and democracy as prime examples of change about which few would argue today. Thus they remain open to additional changes of thought and practice as new situations demand different responses in the light of their faith.

PRIMI'

EW ENG
OOL.

3

Protestant Faiths and American Culture

PROTESTANTISM HOLDS A UNIQUE PLACE IN AMERICAN CULTURE due to its traditionally dominant role. While minority religious traditions have certainly had an impact on American culture, Protestantism has been seen as the major culture-making tradition in America. The role played by other religions is often seen as broadening America from an exclusive Protestant direction. The continuing influences of Protestantism are found at every turn in America, from the clean lines of New England's Congregational churches to the scheduling of weekend activities to avoid competing with Sunday morning worship services.

Observers have seen the public schools as reflecting mainline Protestant values, beginning with the need for Protestant children to be educated so they could read the Bible. Roman Catholics and several other religions developed private school systems to lessen the effect of Protestant values on their youth.

Protestantism has been credited with instilling Americans with the work ethic that has shaped a particularly American ideal: That through hard, honest labor anyone can create a prosperous life for themselves and their families. The religious foundation to the work ethic has supplied patience during lean years and hope that the afterlife will make up for any shortcomings in this life.

Protestantism has also, at least until quite recently, supplied the language and ceremonies that connected otherwise separate elements of the American community. When presidents invoked God to back their causes and when people sang "God Bless America," they called on the Protestant deity. The whole culture still celebrates the Pilgrims' Thanksgiving, and until quite recently city halls were decorated for Christmas. Another example of Protestant influence can be seen in the general culture when people who have made mistakes or committed crimes are called on to confess their failures and ask forgiveness of the public.

Meanwhile, Protestants have in recent years seen their major challenge as responding to the growth of secularism and the drive to remove all religious symbols and language from public life; the need to revise thinking in the light of scientific advances; and the demands of living in a highly pluralistic culture in which Protestant values now have to compete in a diverse religious community.

Protestantism and the Public Schools

As noted in the previous chapter, early American Protestants placed great emphasis on education. This emphasis led not only to the founding of colleges, but to the creation of many elementary and high schools. In the 19th century, church leaders worked for the establishment and development of the public school system. The Puritans produced the first educational textbooks that included catechisms (church teachings that presented the Christian faith in a question and answer format), which children and young people were taught to memorize. John Cotton (1595–1652), a well-known Congregational minister, for example, published his catechism under the title *Spiritual Milk for American Babes*. Early textbooks such as the *New England Primer*, which taught children their ABCs, did so with sentences that also introduced them to Bible verses.

Although not as successful as they had hoped, the Protestants of the colonial era tried to pass their faith on to their children and saw education as a tool in that effort. The Bible, its stories, its people, and its teachings, were integrated into elementary school curriculum, and college students were expected to learn the biblical languages of Greek and Hebrew. Those that did not go on to college were placed with a tradesman who taught them a trade in a pious environment.

PRECEDING PAGE
One school for all
This magazine illustration from the late 19th century shows the typical arrangement of a colonial-era school. A church-approved teacher instructed children of several ages in one room.

SECULAR
Secular means concerned with the worldly, rather than the spiritual aspects of life. Secularism describes the growing influence of worldly matters and the declining influence of religion.

While the children of church members were largely educated in church-supported schools, as America's population swelled in the 19th century, especially in the cities, and many more people were not affiliated with a church, broad public education was placed on the agenda of church leaders. Such educational programs were aimed particularly at the poorer classes.

The Place of Children

In many families prior to the 20th century, children were viewed quite differently than they are today. They were certainly loved, but they were also seen as family assets. From their sixth or seventh year, they were expected to begin to contribute economically to the family. They took over tasks whose completion directly affected the family's income. On the farm, that might include the feeding and care of animals that were being raised for food or for sale, the planting of the garden, or the preparation of firewood. In the city, it often included going to work as an apprentice or, increasingly, working on an assembly line in a factory. Protestants had taken the lead even in the colonial era to create the first Sunday schools—originally schools at which young people who worked six days a week at a job could learn reading, writing, and basic arithmetic.

In the late 19th century, Protestant ministers and lay leaders were very much part of the change in thinking about children that led to the passing of child labor laws. These laws raised the age at which a child and then a youth could be employed, and removed them from dangerous situations (such as operating complicated machinery). Such laws also enabled more children to spend more time in school. Previously, children as young as 6 to 12 years old regularly worked full weeks in factories. By 1900, 18 percent of children from 12 to 16 worked rather than attended school. Today, federal and state laws normally prohibit work by those younger than 14 and place many limitations on any work performed by those 14 to 18 years old.

The change of thinking in American society from a system in which only the few—primarily the children of the wealthy—were educated to one in which the society takes responsibility to provide a basic education to all of its children and youth was, to a significant extent, the product of Protestant leadership working cooperatively with teachers and educational leaders.

EXCERPTS FROM THE PRIMER

Using stories from the Bible, the *New England Primer* taught children their alphabet. Here is how they learned A through F:

In Adam's Fall
We sinned all

Heaven to find
the Bible mind

Christ crucify'd
For sinners dy'd

The Deluge drown'd
The Earth around

Elijah hid,
By Ravens fed

The Judgement made

School Prayer Issues

As public schools came into existence, the Protestant majorities in most communities felt that schools should, on a non-sectarian basis (that is, not favoring one church over the other), reinforce Christian values. It became common to begin the school day with brief patriotic and religious exercises. Through the 20th century, this activity often took the form of saying the pledge of allegiance, a reading from the Bible (a Protestant translation), and a prayer. Criticism of this practice grew in the early 20th century as the country became more pluralistic. In some schools, especially where a large group of students came from non-Christian religions (such as Judaism or Buddhism), opening religious exercises were informally removed.

In the years following World War II, however, criticism of the Christian religious exercises increased. To counter the effects of such criticism, some schools attempted to move to a format that generally affirmed widely held religious beliefs, beyond those that were specifically Christian. For example, in the 1950s the State of New York issued a set of guidelines for the inclusion of moral and spiritual training in the public schools. Attention focused on an ecumenical (promoting unity of religions) prayer that appeared to be quite acceptable not just to Christians but to Jews and Muslims as well:

> Almighty God, we acknowledge our dependence upon Thee, and we beg
> Thy blessings upon us, our parents, our teachers and our Country.

Some parents objected to this prayer and broadened their objection to the inclusion not only of this prayer but of any prayer in the public school day. Since students were, by this time, required to attend school, they argued that it involved the state establishment of religion, which was against the First Amendment (discussed in the previous chapter). The Supreme Court agreed, and in 1962 in a case known as *Engel* v. *Vitale*, the Court declared unconstitutional the inclusion of state-sponsored school prayer as part of any public school curriculum.

Many people, mostly the more conservative element in the Protestant community, were upset over the decision, and since that time have attempted to find an acceptable substitute. However, given the ever-increasing religious diversity in the United States (not to mention the growth of an articulate non-religious community), they have been unable to pose a solution that has overcome the Court's objection.

The reading of the Bible was challenged on the same grounds. Possibly the most important court case was called *Abington v. Schempp*. It was a challenge to 1949 Pennsylvania law that mandated Bible reading in public schools statewide. In 1963, the Supreme Court found that, like prayer, Bible reading also contradicted constitutional provisions against the state-established religion. As with the prayer decision, many Protestants felt that the government had betrayed them, although they accepted the court decision.

The Lutheran Church in America saw the decision of the Court as a call for Christians to do more effective jobs within their own constituency. "This [decision] points up the challenge to the churches and to the public schools to give serious attention to ways of studying the Bible and religion that will do justice to the religious factor and at the same time serve the larger neutrality which an even-handed interpretation of the Constitution requires."

Similar statements to the Lutherans' (see the box below) were issued by other churches. The issue of Bible reading has largely dropped from the debate, but the issue of prayer in schools has become an ongoing debate in American religious circles. This debate has been

A School Prayer Statement

This is an excerpt from a statement by the executive council of the Lutheran Church in America, issued in 1963 in response to several court cases limiting or banning school prayer.

We do not believe that much has been lost in terms of the specific points covered by the recent decisions of the United States Supreme Court in the school prayer and Bible reading cases. If the Lord's Prayer were to be recited in schoolrooms only for the sake of the moral and ethical atmosphere it creates, it would be worth nothing to the practicing Christian. The Lord's Prayer is the supreme act of adoration and petition or it is debased. Reading the Bible in the pub-

lic schools without comment, too, has been of dubious value as either an educational or religious experience. The more we attempt as Christians or Americans to insist on common denominator religious exercise or instruction in public schools, the greater risk we run of diluting our faith and contributing to a vague religiosity which identifies religion with patriotism and becomes a national folk religion.

This event intensifies the task of the church. It heightens the need of the church for strength to stand alone, lofty and unshaken, in American society. It calls for greater depth of conviction in all Christian men and women.

fueled somewhat by a widespread misunderstanding. The court decisions ordered only that public school-sponsored and state-mandated prayer and Bible reading exercises be curtailed. It did not in any way prevent students from engaging in prayer, either privately or as a group, or from reading of the Bible, if they desire. Thus it has been that many student prayer and/or Bible study groups have arisen across the country, especially among high school students. These often meet just before or after the regular school hours or during an activity period in which a variety of student special interest groups meet.

Continuing Protestant Impact on Higher Education

The process of Protestant churches founding schools to train laypeople and provide the churches with clerical leadership has continued to the present. This early emphasis on education eventually permeated the Baptists and Methodists and then almost all of the different denominations. However, meeting the highest educational standards characterized the schools founded by the older Protestant churches, and they would attain a leadership role in higher education.

Through the 19th century, it was common for colleges to secularize. Religion departments separated and/or evolved into modern theological seminaries that retained their relationships to one denomination.

Oberlin Opens Its Doors

Young, idealistic students at newly founded Oberlin College in Ohio made demands of their new teachers—the school was to open its doors to African American students as a matter of policy. The Oberlin faculty and administration agreed to the conditions imposed by the new students and welcomed black students beginning in 1835. By the end of the century, one-third of all of African Americans with degrees from a predominantly white school graduated from Oberlin. The admission of black students undercut objections to the admission of females, and in 1837, the school also opened its doors to women. In 1841, the first three women in America to earn a B.A. degree graduated from Oberlin. As with African Americans, a high percentage of female college graduates through the remainder of the century received their degrees from Oberlin.

Oberlin's importance only grew after theologian/evangelist Charles G. Finney (1792–1875) was attracted to Oberlin as pastor of First Congregational Church. The town and the college became not only the Midwestern center for abolitionist agitation, but also a national center for a generation of moral crusades and social reform.

At the same time, many of the schools founded by the different churches remained as private liberal arts colleges. A few (for example, Carleton College in Northfield, Minnesota) attained national fame for their excellence in training undergraduates. Others, like Oberlin College in Ohio, played an important role in history. Oberlin was founded in 1833. At about the same time, not far away in Cincinnati, Ohio, Lane Theological Seminary, a Presbyterian school, had become the largest ministerial training school in the country. Among its students was Theodore Dwight Weld (1803-1895), who took the lead in a school-wide debate over slavery in 1834. He was an abolitionist, and while finding support among the student body, the majority of the faculty opposed such radical notions. Thus it was that a former trustee of Lane, Asa Mahan, now based at Oberlin, was able to lure the Lane rebels to the new school (see the box opposite).

While few schools have the history of Oberlin, the contribution of Protestant colleges, universities, and seminaries to the building and sustaining of America is truly monumental. From the University of the South in Sawanee, Tennessee (Episcopal) to Pacific Lutheran University in Tacoma, Washington (Lutheran), the Protestant churches have committed themselves to providing sound education and raising up leaders in every corner of the nation. This commitment to education has ensured their retaining an influence in society far beyond that which these churches might otherwise have exercised.

Christian Culture

In Europe, Christian churches commonly saw themselves as maintaining the religious foundation of the broader society. They were concerned not only with spiritual issues, but also with the moral and cultural aspects of secular life. In a similar way, colonial Congregationalists tried to create a Puritan culture in which religion affected all areas of life, and Anglican and Reformed leaders tried to reproduce life as they had known it in Europe, complete with the church's fullest participation.

In the early decades of the United States, given the voluntary contribution system, and the fact that church members made up such a small percentage of the population, the churches felt added incentives were needed to recover their traditional place in society. They had to bring in large numbers of the growing public. Through the entire 19th century growth was spectacular. Immigration of many people from Europe played a big part in this growth, as did continuing efforts by the churches to evangelize, or attract new believers. By the end of the century, membership had doubled and redoubled itself several times over, and the percentage of the public who became members of churches increased from less that 15 percent to more than 30 percent.

As church membership grew, church leaders could also begin to think about the more public aspects of morality and social concerns. Of immediate concern was perceived widespread public immorality, from public drunkenness to unacceptably high crime rates. American church leaders began to found a series of voluntary benevolent societies to address a range of issues. There were anti-slavery societies, temperance societies battling against alcohol use, literacy groups that used Sunday schools to help children learn to read, and groups that worked for prison reform. So extensive was the spread and impact of these societies that by the 1840s people could speak of the "Benevolent Empire" whose goal was building a Christian civilization in North America.

If a Christian civilization was to be built, then the unbelieving public would have to be won. Thus it was that a set of organizations was created to win the world for Christ. In 1814 Justin Edwards (1787-1853) of Andover Theological Seminary in Connecticut founded the

New England Tract Society to publish Christian literature. It became the seed that led in 1925 to the formation of the American Tract Society (still in existence), which in its first decade produced and distributed more than 1 million pieces of literature.

Another Andover graduate, Samuel J. Mills (1783–1818), helped found the American Bible Society, which specialized in printing and distributing inexpensive editions of the Bible. Today, the society is still operating and produces Bibles in many languages for distribution in America and most countries of the world.

Efforts to Convert Jewish Americans

Two efforts of the Benevolent Empire have been the source of persistent criticism, especially through the 20th century: the societies founded to convert Jews and Native Americans. The relationship between the Jewish and Christian communities over the centuries has been marred by Christian attempts to forcibly convert Jews. Anti-Jewish propaganda freely circulated in the Christian societies of Europe.

In America, the original Jewish community was relatively small—some 8,000 people—and of little interest to the Protestant churches. However, in 1820, a small gift was made to the Presbyterian Church to commence a ministry to Jews. It was not immediately acted upon, but in 1846 a young theological student was commissioned to start such a ministry which blossomed among the many German Jews then emigrating to the United States.

While facing their ups and downs, Presbyterian-sponsored centers set up to convert Jews spread across the United States over the next decade. Through the rest of the century, Jewish missions were founded by most churches, Protestant and otherwise, and their work was reinforced by a number of independent missionary organizations that drew support from a cross-section of churches.

In the early 20th century, the Jewish community organized structures to oppose efforts to convert them, and supported the initial efforts to create a dialogue between the Jewish and Christian communities. Such agencies as the National Conference of Christians and Jews (now the National Conference for Community and Justice) pioneered understanding between the two groups.

In the years after World War II, a whole new relationship was created between the two communities, primarily as a result of the

Holocaust, in which 6 million Jews were killed by the Nazis for no other reason than that they were born Jewish. As the details of the suffering and death of the Jewish people during Holocaust reached the Protestant churches, they collectively acknowledged their part in allowing such an event to happen, both by not standing up against it as it was occurring and by perpetuating negative images of Jews in centuries of anti-Semitic literature, much of it written by Protestant Christians.

In the years since World War II, almost all Protestant churches have discontinued support for missionary efforts especially targeting the Jewish community. Nonetheless, such missions continue, but they are largely supported by independent evangelical organizations that draw support from individual local churches. Several of the more conservative Protestant bodies continue Jewish missions, most notably the Lutheran Church-Missouri Synod and the smaller Wisconsin Evangelical Lutheran Synod.

In place of Jewish missions, most of the larger Protestant groups have been very active in an ongoing dialogue with the Jewish community. This dialogue is aimed at addressing past grievances the Jewish community feels it has suffered, building structures that will prevent anything like the Holocaust from ever occurring again, and engaging in a dialogue about the state of Israel. Israel has been the object of the most intense discussions between Protestant and Jewish leaders, as Protestants have tried to also sympathize with Palestinians in the troubled Middle East.

Converting Native Americans

As with the Jewish community, Protestant relations with Native Americans have also been fraught with difficulties. The churches supported the European conquest of North America. As European settlement advanced, religious leaders showed a lack of understanding of the reaction of Native Americans to the destruction of their livelihood and traditional ways of life. More often than not they treated Native American people as at best childlike and more frequently as hopeless savages.

During the colonial era, Native Americans became active players in the power struggles of the French and British for control of the continent.

During this period, several attempts had been made to evangelize Native Americans—a few successful, others ending in disaster. The most famous mission was founded by Congregational minister John Eliot (1604–1690). At the beginning of the 1650s, after several years of preaching to the Indians who resided near his church at Roxbury, Massachusetts, he founded the first of what were known as "praying towns," settlements of Christian converts. He established more than a dozen similar communities and translated the Bible into the local languages. These towns never became strong Christian communities, however. Like most Puritans, Eliot could not understand why the Indians would want to become Christians without also wanting to adopt the "superior" European culture.

This inability to understand the values of Native American culture informed both the government's Indian policy through the 19th century and the church's participation in it. In 1819, for example, the government established an acculturation fund to provide resources for Native Americans to adapt to the European way of life. Missionaries joined the government payroll as farmers and teachers so that Christianity would be taught along with the more secular subjects aimed at moving Native American Americans into the now-dominant European culture.

In the 1820s, missionaries working in the Southern states noted great success among the Cherokees, Creeks, Choctaws, and Chickasaws, who began to adapt to the new reality to the point that they became known as the "civilized" tribes. This effort ended, however, when gold was discovered in Georgia and the government mandated the removal of Native Americans west of the Mississippi River in the late 1820s. Over the next several decades, the U.S. government forcibly removed Native American tribes from numerous states and territories, claiming their land for the new nation. The tribes were removed to "reservations," often many miles from their original home. This process of removal sometimes was peaceful, but at other times it was quite violent and bloody.

Numerous are the stories of missionaries acting to the detriment of those among whom they worked, though they are balanced by the accounts of missionaries rising to the occasion. The career of Samuel Worcester (1798-1859), a Presbyterian minister in Georgia, illustrates the latter. When the government demanded the Cherokee leave their land, Worcester protested and was arrested. His case finally came before the Supreme Court in 1831, and the court ruled in favor of the Cherokee Nation, that the government did not have the right to displace them. In spite of the Supreme Court ruling, most of the Cherokee were ultimately removed, but Worcester's protest is partially credited with the Cherokee maintaining some continuing presence in their traditional homeland. Through the rest of the century, missionaries increasingly emerged as a buffer between the Native American people and those government policies and secular forces that continually tried to steal even the land left to Native Americans in the reservations.

The churches kept trying to work with to Native Americans through the period when the reservation system was established. As missionaries became more culturally sophisticated, they were more capable of identifying with the people, though for many years the issue of education remained an irritant. Missionaries valued Western style education, while through most of the 19th century, Native American people, who had a sophisticated but nonliterary culture, did not. Missionaries also tended to use a boarding-school model, which often separated children from their parents and other members of their community for many months at a time.

In the end, the missionaries had a massive effect on Native American life and the majority of Native Americans became Christians, though spread out among a variety of denominations, including Catholic and Mormon.

Finding the Radio Audience

Well into the 20th century, the printed page remained the primary means of communicating the message of the Christian churches to members and nonmembers alike, and it still remains a vital element. However, in 1920, a new medium of expression became available—radio.

The first licensed radio station in America went on the air in Pittsburgh, Pennsylvania, in November 1920. The first religious radio broadcast occurred just two months later on that same station with the airing of an evening vesper (prayer) service from Calvary Episcopal Church on January 2, 1921. Audience response led to the services being broadcast weekly. As other stations opened around the country, they integrated religious broadcasts into their regular schedule almost from the first day.

Broadcasting was an unregulated enterprise for the next six years with a wide variety of religious groups becoming involved, some even buying their own radio stations. Then, in 1927, the newly created

Rolling the Presses

Protestantism's efforts to create a literate membership and raise the reading level of the general public also created people who would read the books and periodicals that many churches began to produce. Among the first of the benevolent associations to emerge in the 19th century were the American Tract Society and the American Bible Society.

Through the 19th century, increasing access to printing presses enabled the churches to produce vast quantities of literature. Not only did each church have its national periodicals, but state and local units also produced newspapers and magazines. Within the larger denominations, dissenting groups were also relatively free to publish, and publications such as broadsides, booklets, and journals became the instruments through which debates on a wide selection of topics took place. Among the issues discussed were slavery, war and peace, the spread of the Mormon religion, Roman Catholicism, colonization, western expansion, and much more.

Federal Radio Commission (FRC) laid down the first set of regulations. The FRC was superseded in 1934 by the Federal Communications Commission. The larger denominations, speaking through the Federal Council of Churches, took the occasion to propose a new policy for radio broadcasting—at least for those stations now aligned with the two major radio networks. Instead of radio stations selling time to anyone who could buy it, the churches proposed that no time be sold to any religious groups.

Rather, each station should allocate a certain amount of time each week to religious programming, and that time should be parceled out exclusively to the major Protestant, Catholic, and Jewish organizations. CBS and NBC agreed to that proposal, and independent groups, including many conservative Fundamentalists, were limited to purchasing time from the remaining independent stations and the other network, the Mutual Broadcasting System. Then the Mutual Broadcasting System adopted the same policy as ABC and NBC, and independent religious broadcasters shifted almost entirely to independent stations.

Peale on the Air

One exception to the tendency of Protestant churches to avoid television was the work developed by Reformed Church in America ministers Norman Vincent Peale (1898-1993, right) and Robert Schuller (b. 1926). Peale, the pastor of Marble Collegiate Church in New York City for many years, had become a national celebrity after writing a best-selling book, *The Power of Positive Thinking*, in 1952. He spent the rest of his life building on ideas first explored there. For more than 40 years, beginning in the 1930s, Peale hosted "The Art of Living" radio show, and made the transition to television in the 1950s. The common-sense, upbeat messages of the show resonated with millions of listeners and viewers. Real success on television, however, came to his successor, Schuller, who continues his own version of Peale's message in "The Hour of Power" broadcast. It began in 1970 and by the 1990s was one of the most popular religious television shows on the air, combining positive Christian messages with music, performance, and a beautiful setting in the Crystal Cathedral in Garden Grove, California.

Turning Off Television

After World War II, most of the larger denominations in America united in the new National Council of Churches (which replaced the former Federal Council). The formation of the Council in 1950 came just as television was about to open still another medium for spreading the word, and the Council recommended that the radio networks extend their policy in religious broadcasting to television. The effect of this policy was to limit religious television for the next 20 years.

The attempt of the larger churches to control religious radio and television began to fall apart in the 1970s. Although television stations continued to offer free time for religious programming, they also began to sell time to whoever could pay for it.

The spread of television, and the appearance of television personalities such as Pentecostal minister Oral Roberts and Southern Baptist preacher Billy Graham, led many in the mainline churches to openly oppose the use of television as an arm of the church's ministry. They argued that such an impersonal medium, offering a form of Christianity divorced from involvement in church life, contrasted with the personal religious life that was the ideal of a Christian community. They failed to see the role of television as a supplement to the spirituality of active Christians and a meaningful ministry to the homebound.

A few broadcast ministries backed by the older churches continued to keep the churches' feet in the waters of broadcast ministry, the most notable being "The Protestant Hour" backed by Lutherans. However, overwhelmingly in the 1980s, both radio and television religious broadcasting was dominated by independent ministers and teachers from the smaller evangelical and conservative churches. There were a few notable broadcasts from groups of the conservative Christian Reformed Church; the Lutheran Church-Missouri Synod's "The Lutheran Hour" remains one of the most popular religious radio shows ever.

While religious broadcasting is still dominated by independent Evangelicals, recently the more mainline churches have joined their efforts with the National Interfaith Cable Coalition, an association of Christian and Jewish groups dedicated to producing television programming. The coalition prepares shows for the new Faith and Values Network, which is aired nationally on the Hallmark cable channel. The Coalition includes 31 member groups that have a total combined membership of 120 million.

Into All the World

One of the most frequently repeated stories in American Christian history concerns young Samuel J. Mills (1783-1818), who attended Williams College and while there organized a secret society that gathered regularly at a maple grove near campus for prayer and the discussion of pressing issues of faith. One day in 1806, on their way to the grove, members were caught in a sudden thunderstorm and took shelter under a haystack. As the rain continued they prayed for the non-Christian world and resolved that they would go out into the world as America's first foreign missionaries. Some members of this group subsequently attended Andover Theological Seminary, where they formed another group, the Society of Inquiry on the Subject of Missions.

In 1810, four of the group presented themselves before the General Association of Congregational Ministers of Massachusetts to argue their case for missions. As a result, the Association founded the American Board of Commissioners for Foreign Missions. This board was to bring the first group of Americans into the foreign missionary program that had begun in England in the previous century, and would become one of the most important missionary organizations of the next century. Through the efforts of the American Board, and a similar board that would be organized by the other Protestant churches in the next decades. Protestantism mobilized its membership during the 19th century and sent missionaries to almost every country on the globe. At the beginning of the century, Protestantism was largely confined to Western and Northern Europe and the Eastern half of North America. By the end of the 19th century it had a substantial presence on every continent. It had become a worldwide faith.

Interestingly enough, Mills did not become a missionary and stayed in America to organize a variety of benevolent societies, including the aforementioned American Bible Society.

The Mission of the Missions Changes

American Protestants joined with their European counterparts to create the global missionary movement. Numerous missions were set up in the South Pacific; in Asia from India and Sri Lanka to Japan and Korea; and in every part of Africa. As the churches moved overseas, they carried with them all the issues that had divided them into Lutherans and Anglicans and Reformed and Congregationalists. In some cases these issues continued to divide, but in many cases they were overcome to produce new united Protestant churches, and in most cases led to cooperative councils that worked to minimize the effects of differences between the different churches.

By the beginning of the 20th century, the larger Protestant churches in America had created substantial support for missionaries in many countries around the globe. However, through the 20th century, the missionary situation would change as dramatically as it had in the previous century.

As the missionary enterprise expanded, missionaries became much more aware of the cultural disruption that had occurred due to the expectation that converts would also adopt European ways. This realization led the missions to develop leadership from among their converts and to push various national missions to develop into autonomous churches.

This trend was also in line with the change of opinion concerning colonialism and the granting of independence to almost all of the European colonies in the years after World War II. Through the last half of the 20th century, the missions of most American Protestant churches dropped their mission status and became independent church

Spreading the word
Christian missionaries, such as this man in Ecuador, have taken their faith from America to every continent on earth.

bodies. American churches continued to assist former missions with both personnel and financial means, but now as equal partners in the world missionary enterprise.

Many of these newer churches united with their parent bodies in the World Council of Churches. Thus American Protestant churches, once large international bodies, again became national churches, but with significant worldwide networks to sister churches in other countries. Through these former mission churches, the Protestant churches remade the religious configuration of the majority of the world in the 19th and 20th century.

Protestant Faiths and Social Issues

AS THE RELIGION OF THE MAJORITY IN AMERICA, PROTESTANTISM'S involvement in social issues has frequently mirrored the concerns and debates over social change that have dominated the country at any given moment. At their best, Protestants have tended to lead in projecting a vision of a just and loving society, and at their worst to reinforce prejudices and outworn social structures. These two sides are somewhat related to the two sometimes conflicting realities of the religious Protestant life. On one hand, churches are by their nature conservative institutions that exist to perpetuate traditional Christian values, which include community, service, personal moral responsibility, and stable social structures. On the other hand, Christian churches look for the coming kingdom of God and see this life as preparation for the future kingdom. Protestant churches, in particular, consider themselves as being in a continual state of reformation. This aspect of Protestant life offers a path to criticism of both church and society, and can at times lead to disruptions of social structures as it demands a more just society and a church more responsive to the needs of people.

Many Christians have adopted a more conservative outlook, emphasizing the need for stable structures (law and order) and giving high priority to issues of personal morality and ethics. More liberal Christians have

PRECEDING PAGE
Carrying the load
Inspired by their religious convictions, many Protestant leaders joined the fight for civil rights for African Americans in the 1960s, such as this unidentified Episcopal minister, who carries a child during a 1963 protest outside the United Nations in New York.

identified with various alienated communities in American life. They have worked for the inclusion of all in the shared social structures and to create conditions by which whole groups of people can have the resources to assume a responsible place in the social order.

Differences in this basic approach to the Christian life have led to a variety of heated debates within the larger church bodies, and on occasion, as decisions have been made, have led to the losing group leaving and forming a separate denomination. In the 19th century, several churches (including the Presbyterians) split over the issue of slavery. In the early 20th century, schisms occurred over a variety of issues that included both theological concerns and the approach to social change. As a result of church splits in the 1930s, the more liberal voices came to dominate most of the larger Protestant bodies (the Lutheran Church-Missouri Synod and the Christian Reformed Churches being prominent exceptions).

We do not have the space to discuss more than a small sample of the issues that have concerned the Protestant churches over the last two centuries, but the four discussed here illustrate some of the more important concerns of the last generation.

From Slavery to Civil Rights

Possibly the most important social issue since the birth of the nation in which the church and American society have interacted has been race. Slavery had been established in America in the colonial era, when hundreds of thousands of African people were brought forcibly to the Americas, especially to work the plantations. The system, having been approved by the Constitution, expanded in the early 19th century. By the 1830s competing economic forces in the growing nation and the moral questions concerning human bondage had combined to place slavery before the public as the number one issue.

Protestant church leaders could be found on all sides of the debate. Some, especially in the South where slavery was most extensive, built strong cases for continuing slavery. After all, slavery is mentioned in several places in the Old and New Testaments, and there is no call in scripture for its abolition. Church leaders who supported slavery tried to introduce Christianity to the plantation (often against owners' objections) and until it was specifically outlawed, they taught the basics of reading and writing. The Methodists and Baptists were most successful in this effort, and to this day most African Americans identify with one of those churches.

Some Protestants, largely in New England and various Midwestern cities, championed abolition—the immediate end to slavery. This argument was based primarily on moral considerations combined with a reading of the Bible that emphasized passages in support of freedom. Paul's admonition that "In Christ there is no Jew nor Greek, no bond nor free, no male nor female, for you are one in Jesus Christ," (Galatians 3:28) was a favorite passage.

Abolitionists organized societies to advance their cause and published numerous books, tracts, and periodicals. The Oberlin

John Brown's Example

Protestants, Quakers, and other abolitionists joined in the creation of the Underground Railroad, a system of safe houses that provided shelters and hiding places for escaping slaves to make their way to permanent freedom in Canada. Typical of those who risked their lives and fortunes were Presbyterian minister John Rankin and his wife Jean, who organized their neighbors in Ripley, Ohio, and are credited with assisting thousands of slaves to find freedom. Their home, one stop on the Underground Railroad, became known as Liberty Hill.

But even this work was not enough for a few, and in 1859, one Congregationalist layman, John Brown (1800–1859, right), accompanied by Presbyterian minister Paul Hill and a small band of recruits, entered the history books when they seized the Federal arsenal in Harpers Ferry, Virginia. Brown hoped to launch an insurrection of slaves, but after the group was captured, he and his co-conspirators were treated as criminals, and he was hanged. Brown, remembered today for being ultimately on the winning side, said he acted on a mandate from God.

evangelists, for example (see page 60), regularly demanded that their audience immediately renounce all involvement in slavery.

Encountering significant resistance, especially after the Fugitive Slave Law of 1850 (which gave slave owners the right to travel into non-slave states to recover runaway slaves), abolitionists adopted more aggressive actions to assist slaves, such as the Underground Railroad that secretly helped slaves escape. Abolitionists also supported slave-led actions such as the 1831 rebellion led by slave Nat Turner (1800–1831), which ended with Turner's capture.

By far the largest percentage of Protestant leaders fell into the anti-slavery camp, meaning they opposed slavery, but looked for various programs by which it could be eliminated gradually without undue harm to either the country's economy or the financial condition of slave owners. Anti-slavery people tended to view abolitionists as radical fanatics, and on several occasions the more radical voices were pushed out of the larger churches.

Forward from the Civil War

The Civil War (1860–1865) ended the slavery debate. As a result of the war, the abolitionist cause was vindicated and slavery abolished. Some churches (Methodists, Baptists, and Presbyterians) had split as the war approached, and the broken fellowships would be continued for the long term. However, all of the churches, both in the former free states and the former Confederacy now had to respond to the needs of the newly freed African Americans.

For the Methodists and Baptists, the response primarily took the form of assisting the establishment of independent denominational structures. For the older Protestant churches, none of whom had a significant African-American membership, it meant the beginning of efforts to help newly freed citizens take advantage of their situation. The most important tool the churches had to offer was education, and during the decades after the Civil War numerous church-based schools at all levels of educational need were formed.

The Protestant churches built small but significant memberships in the African-American communities over the next century. During this time, a set of discriminatory laws put into place a segregated society. While most visible in the South, where segregation of blacks was

BACK TO AFRICA?

Among the anti-slavery efforts was recolonization, a program that advocated the return of Africans to their homeland. Through the years of its existence, the American Colonization Society, founded in 1816 by Robert Finley (1772–1817), financed passage for more than 13,000 Africans to move to West Africa, to what in 1847 became the nation of Liberia.

written into law, segregation was also active across the United States with African Americans being forced into segregated neighborhoods in most American cities.

Demands for an end to segregation picked up strength following World War II and the return of many soldiers who had seen the relative lack of racial barriers in other countries. Then, in 1948, a Supreme Court ruling began the process of desegregating public schools. A further challenge to segregated living that began with the 1956 bus boycott in Montgomery, Alabama, erupted into the Civil Rights movement. Following the non-violent philosophy articulated by Baptist minister Martin Luther King, Jr. (1929–1968), the movement mobilized leaders across the spectrum of the religious community nationwide. Protestant ministers marched beside Unitarian activists, Jewish rabbis locked arms with Catholic priests, Baptist preachers sang freedom songs with humanist teachers.

No one religious community can claim credit above the others for their effort on behalf of Civil Rights. The movement was generated within the African-American community, who took the lead, and the role of the churches became one essentially of reacting to the movement's existence. However, the support of so many Protestant leaders and their organizations, such as the National Council of Churches, certainly facilitated the speedy passage of the Civil Rights Act. The presence of Protestant church leaders from the highest levels, and the inclusion of so many Protestants in the 1963 March on Washington, assured political leaders of the popular support they needed to pass the legislation in 1965.

Civil Rights in the Churches

The rise of the Civil Rights movement not only mobilized the churches in what became a popular moral crusade, but forced them to confront the racial structures, both formal and informal, in their own organizations. Even as Civil Rights were being codified as public law, the churches began to deal with the informal structures that had made African Americans second-class members in the larger Protestant bodies. This issue came to the fore in the late 1960s, and took many forms in the different churches.

In the Episcopal Church, a notable landmark came in 1970 when a black bishop, John Burgess, was appointed for the first time in the

FIGHT FOR CIVIL RIGHTS

The national fight for equal rights for Americans of all races began in earnest in Montgomery, Alabama. A 1956 citywide boycott of buses followed the 1955 arrest of bus rider Rosa Parks (b.1913) for not moving to the back of the bus, as was the law and custom for African Americans. The boycott was international news and one of the first significant events in the Civil Rights Movement.

Led by religious leaders of all faiths, the movement spread across the South and then the nation, leading to numerous demonstrations, protests, and confrontations with police. On August 28, 1963, hundreds of thousands of people, mostly African American, took part in the March on Washington. In front of this crowd and before a worldwide television audience, Martin Luther King, Jr., gave the most famous speech of the era: "I Have a Dream." he called for a society that "judged people not by the color of their skin but by the content of their character."

Spurred to action by these events, Congress passed the Civil Rights Act in 1965, which guaranteed equal protection under the law for Americans of all races.

United States with authority over predominantly white congregations. Three years later a commission for African-American ministries was established as a continuing voice for black Episcopalians within the church.

The majority of Lutherans at the time of the Civil Rights movement were in the American Lutheran Church and the Lutheran Church in America. Having been largely based in northern European American ethnic communities, there were few black members; however, associations were formed in both Lutheran groups to encourage and ensure full participation for African-American members.

Presbyterians, who had the longest history of participation in improving the lot of African Americans, finally elected Elder G. Hawkins as the first black moderator (senior council member) of what was then called the United Presbyterian Church in 1964. It would be a decade later before its southern counterpart would follow suit. Since the two churches merged in 1983, a National Black Presbyterian Caucus has kept members aware of the African-American minority in their midst.

The Status and Role of Women

As we have seen, Protestant churches often reflect mainstream American culture. This is certainly illustrated in the new role assumed by women in church life in the 20th century. While some churches, most notably the Holiness and Pentecostal churches, had moved women into ministerial leadership positions early in the 20th century, the mainline Protestant churches were much slower to act.

Most Protestant churches recognize two orders of ordained clergy: elders (variously known as presbyters, priests, or ministers) and deacons. Elders are ordained to preach the Gospel and lead in sacramental services (baptism and Communion). Deacons (the word means "one who serves") specialize in ministries of compassion, helpfulness, and assistance to those in need. All elders have been ordained as deacons, but Protestant churches also support the work of a permanent diaconate. The Episcopal Church recognizes the episcopate (primarily monks and nuns) as a third order of ministry.

The Episcopal Church ordained the first woman to the diaconate in 1920, but it wasn't until 1974 that the first women were ordained as priests. This ordination occurred outside of normal channels, even as the church was locked in heated debate over the issue. Three bishops,

Robert L. DeWitt, Edward Welles, and Daniel Corrigan, each either retired or resigned from their diocese, joined with Antonio Ramos, bishop of Puerto Rico, who served as a witness, in the ordination of 11 women, some of whom had waited for a number of years for the church to let them in. The ordination of the "Philadelphia 11" took place in the Church of the Advocate in Philadelphia on a hot Monday morning, July 29. In spite of the sweltering heat, the church was packed.

These irregular ordinations were officially approved two years later and inspired the church to finally welcome women into the ordained ministry. Fourteen years later, in 1988, the Diocese of Massachusetts elected Barbara C. Harris, an African American, as the Episcopal Church's first female bishop. However, before Harris took office, conservatives in the church, already upset over what they saw as too many wrong turns in church policies, decided the church's decision on ordination had gone too far. Acknowledging the irreversible change that occurred with the welcoming of women into the priesthood, they found bishops who supported their rejection of women priests and who were willing to consecrate bishops for a "continuing church." They split from the Episcopal Church. However, they also proved unable to hold their movement together and it splintered into a variety of small conservative Anglican bodies.

The fact that all of the clergy mentioned in the Bible were male and that an all-male clergy had been perpetuated through the centuries

The United Church of Christ, which continues the Congregationalist tradition in America, has a unique history. Because it placed many issues, including ordination, in the hands of the congregations, Congregationalists ordained their first female minister in 1850. A precocious child, Antoinette Brown Blackwell (1825–1921) had begun to address groups publicly in her local Congregational church when she was only nine years old. She graduated from Oberlin College in 1847 and then completed the theological course of study in 1850 (though even Oberlin did not grant her a degree). In like measure, no church ordained her, but she was able to become the pastor of the Congregationalist church in South Butler, New York. She had to wait three years, but was finally ordained in 1853. Her ordination did not start a trend, and few would follow her over the next century. However, she had set a precedent, and when women found a receptive congregation there would be no barrier from the denomination.

have been sufficient reasons for most conservative Protestants to oppose the ordination of women. Churches such as the Lutheran Church-Missouri Synod continue to hold that position. However, as early as 1926, Lutherans in the Netherlands broke with that tradition and began ordaining women. Other Lutheran churches in Europe followed suit in the decades after World War II. The debate within the larger American Lutheran bodies culminated in 1970 when both the American Lutheran Church and the Lutheran Church in America (today united as the Evangelical Lutheran Church in America) voted to ordain women.

Two Divisive Issues

The role of women in the church is, in many ways, related to two issues that currently have the attention of all of the major denominations: homosexuality and abortion. Actions and thoughts on both issues can best be understood in light of the earlier reaction to women's ordination. Many felt, for example, that the acknowledgement of women as ordained ministers was an attack on family life and women's roles as wife and mother. Similarly, the debate on homosexuality has been fueled by traditional Protestant assumptions about the centrality of family life. And while the churches' admonitions about sexual behavior have been ignored by some and broken by many, the churches have spoken in a united voice that sexual activity should be limited to married couples. Through the last half of the 20th century, numerous voices have arisen to challenge that position. The arguments of the homosexual community have been heard most loudly.

Protestants and the Gay Community

Since the 1960s, the homosexual community, which now includes gay men, lesbians, bisexuals, and transgendered people (often abbreviated GLBT), has convinced many that homosexuals are different at birth and that it is unfair to force their sexual life into a heterosexual mode. They have become quite visible since the 1960s, there being predomi-

Wave of the future
Episcopal priests and their supporters gathered on the steps of the Cathedral of St. John of the Wilderness before a Eucharist service marking an Episcopal gathering in Denver in 2000.

nantly-GLBT communities in most urban areas and many GLBT organizations on college and university campuses. GLBT people have demanded acceptance in many quarters, including the churches.

The GLBT community has also been affected dramatically by the spread of AIDS, a sexually transmitted disease that initially claimed most of its victims in America among GLBT people and continues to affect that group disproportionately. AIDS is particularly devastating in that there is, to date, no cure. It has given rise to many labeling AIDS as a gay disease and those religious leaders most opposed to the GLBT community claiming it is God's curse on those who practice sex outside of marriage. All the major Protestant churches, both liberal and conservative, have flatly rejected such opinions.

In dealing with homosexual concerns, the larger churches have spoken with unanimity on many issues. They welcome members of the GLBT community into their memberships and view them as equals, usually stated as seeing all GLBT individuals, like all people, as chil-

The Gay Marriage Issue

The acceptance of homosexual people for ordination is closely related to the second issue—gay marriage. It should be noted that in America, marriage is a secular affair. That is, the state regulates marriage, issuing marriage licenses to those who meet its criteria and selecting the officials who perform marriages. Of course, in most places, any minister of a duly recognized church may operate as an agent of the state and conduct marriage ceremonies.

In the United States, at present, the government does not recognize the possibility of a marriage being formed by couple in which both people are the same gender. As of 2002, some 25 states have passed legislation that bans same-sex marriage, and additional states were considering it. No state will currently issue a license for a same-sex marriage nor allow one to be registered. While many states have moved to recognize a variety of close, intimate relationships outside of marriage, even allowing many of the benefits of marriage, marriage itself has been denied.

In light of the debate, many gay couples have asked for the recognition of what are termed "unions," a marriage-like relationship into which gay or lesbian couples can enter and which will carry many of the benefits of marriage. In 2000, the state of Vermont passed legislation allowing such unions, and other states are considering the idea. To date, while large minorities favor church ministers officiating at such unions, Protestant churches have yet to give their ministers the go-ahead. Officiating at such unions runs counter to the stated Protestant approval of sexual relationships only within marriage.

dren of God standing in need of God's grace. They have called upon the many medical facilities operated by their churches to be open and compassionate in ministering to people with AIDS. They have also generally supported full civil rights for GLBT people in the secular society and have generally opposed legislative initiatives to curtail them.

However, two issues have been more difficult to resolve. Protestants through the end of the 20th century have been conflicted about admitting practicing homosexuals to the ordained ministry. For the last 30 years, almost every national meeting of the several churches has debated the issue. The more liberal wings of the churches are firmly committed to ordination; the more conservative wings are staunchly opposed; and the large undecided group in the middle is unwilling yet to make any changes.

Certainly many homosexuals have been ordained, overwhelmingly without admitting their sexual orientation ahead of time, including some in the first group of female Episcopalian priests. And a few actions have been taken to push the churches to act, such as the 1973 ordination of William Johnson, the first openly gay male to be ordained in a Protestant church (United Church of Christ), followed in 1977 by the ordination of the first open lesbian, Anne Holmes, in the same church.

The Episcopal Church has come the closest to approving the ordination of gay and lesbian candidates for the priesthood. Several bishops have defied the church by ordaining them as deacons, and no action has been taken to defrock (withdraw authority from) ministers identified as gay after ordination. In 1996, the Episcopal Church court decided that church doctrine does not in and of itself bar ordination of practicing homosexuals. Several dioceses have made official statements in support of ordaining homosexuals.

In 1993, more than 70 percent of the Presbyterian Church (USA)'s General Assembly voted to continue denying lesbian/gay ordinations. However, by the end of the century, an increasing acceptance of gay people has been noted and has led many to predict that the Church will accept gays and lesbians for ordination in the near future.

Protestants and Abortion

Abortion has joined homosexuality as the most divisive issues within the Protestant churches. The question is a modern one, arising as a result of medical advances that have made abortions relatively safe and quick. Abortion, which had been generally outlawed in most states, emerged as an underground industry in the middle of the 20th century as a growing number of doctors came to feel that it should be made available. As a debate developed on the issue, the public became informed of the history of abortion and the extent to which many women would go to have one. They also became aware of the many deaths caused by amateurish and improperly supervised abortions. This information became widely available just as women were making gains both in secular life and in the church.

The issue came to a head in 1973 when the Supreme Court struck down most anti-abortion laws as unconstitutional in the landmark case of *Roe v. Wade*. At this point many conservative Protestant churches and the Roman Catholic Church joined together in their mutual opposition to the practice. The Catholic Church had long opposed abortion as interfering with the natural process of the birth of children. The smaller conservative Evangelical churches equated the practice to the murder of babies, and moved forward with what amounted to a crusade to protect the unborn.

Thus, it was within the large Protestant churches that the debate on abortion took place. Both pro-life (opposing abortion) and pro-choice (favoring a woman's right to choose abortion) groups exist in strength in these churches. The debate has been extended due to the existence of clinics that specialize in abortions and the willingness of pro-life forces to maintain long-term public protests at these clinics.

Within the churches, the debate has become polarized, but nevertheless a broad spectrum of opinion has emerged. On one end are those pro-lifers who are opposed to all abortions under any circumstances. On the other end are those pro-choice people who argue that a woman should have total control over the process, since it is her body that is affected. This position has many sympathizers among people who have worked for women's rights in general and who understand the centuries in which women's lives were largely ruled by male relatives—the same males who made the rules on abortion.

However, in between are many shades of opinion. For example, there are people in Protestant churches who are basically pro-choice, but feel that decisions about abortion are so serious and so affected by individual circumstances, that they should be made by women in consultation with a physician, especially if the pregnant woman is a minor.

WHAT IS *ROE V. WADE*?

That is the name of the 1973 U.S. Supreme Court decision that ruled that abortion is legal in the United States. That decision has been hotly debated ever since. On one side are "pro-life" supporters, who are against abortion and who seek to limit abortions or make them illegal. On the other are "pro-choice" supporters, who feel it is the woman's right to choose and that right should not be restricted.

One Protestant Point of View

Concerning abortion, the General Synod of the Reformed Church in America adopted the following statement in 1973 (taken from the minutes of that meeting):

We believe the Bible teaches the sanctity of human life. Men are given the precious gift of life from God and are created in the image of God. Therefore, we believe, in principle, that abortion ought not to be practiced at all. However, in this complex society, where many times one form of evil is pitted against another form of evil, there could be exceptions. It is our Christian conviction that abortion performed for personal reasons to insure individual convenience ought not to be permitted.

We call on all who counsel those with problem pregnancies, especially youth workers, campus pastors, and staff members of our church colleges, to uphold the Christian alternatives to abortion.

We call on our churches to expand their efforts to support agencies providing a ministry of mercy to those seeking alternatives to abortion.

We call on our members to support efforts for constitutional changes to provide legal protection for the unborn. The gravity of the situation today precludes the possibility of silence at this synod.

There are people who are basically pro-life, but feel that there are some circumstances that justify abortion, most notably when a pregnancy has resulted from a rape or when specific diseases are detected in the baby. Others want to take into account the age of the fetus when the abortion is performed.

In general, the Protestant churches have opted for a pro-choice position, while shying away from endorsing what is termed "abortion on demand." At the same time, they have also opposed the related Roman Catholic position on birth control (totally opposed to all forms of it). Most Protestant churches supported the spread of birth control measures as the most effective way to curtail the need for abortions. At the same time, Protestant churches have also almost unanimously backed programs to promote birth control measures to slow the spread of AIDS.

Conclusion

As these issues show, just as there are a wide variety of Protestant denominations and churches operating in America, there are a wide variety of opinions and courses of action on important societal issues of the day. All these positions are taken by people who feel they are guided by their faiths and beliefs.

5

Protestants and Politics

PROTESTANT INVOLVEMENT IN POLITICS THROUGH THE COLONIAL era followed European models that saw the church and state acting together to build a stable and just social order. These models were shaken at their roots by the separation of church and state mandated by the United States Constitution and the related rulings of the Supreme Court. Under the new system, no church was to be considered part of the state or be financed by the government through taxation.

The new system meant that churches were able to operate with a heightened degree of freedom from political control and influence, since their financial support was no longer dependent on affirming government policies or leadership. In accepting this new leadership, the churches were to refrain from politics by throwing their considerable organizations behind particular candidates or parties.

What the older Protestant churches did carry into the new political system was an understanding of their role in the development of society as a whole. They believed that God had created humans as social animals and that it was God's work to see that a just society developed. This opinion was often not shared by the newer churches, which frequently considered their work to be limited to individuals and the nurturing of their spiritual life. Many conservative Evangelical churches that emerged in the 20th century placed no priority on social ethics and, until the most recent generation, tended to be apolitical (not engaged in political issues).

The separation of church and state, of course, was never absolute. For example, the churches, while separate from the state, cannot operate outside of or in defiance of the law. If church leaders break the law, they are subject to arrest and trial. On the other hand, church members, even ministers, may run for public office, and many do. For example, Mike Huckabee, the governor of Arkansas, is a Baptist minister and graduate of the Southwestern Baptist Theological Seminary. Churches may also participate in the legislative process, and many support lobbying activities directed toward both the national and state legislatures concerning laws of particular concern to them.

Friends in High Places

The primary influence exerted by Protestant churches on the national political scene has been through their many members who have been elected to high office. Though only a relatively small percentage of the population are members of the older, mainline Protestant churches, a disproportionate number of national political figures have been drawn from their ranks. For example, of the 42 people who have been president of the United States, 12 have been Episcopalians. Compare that to the less than 1 percent of the population that is currently affiliated with the Episcopal Church. The most recent Episcopalian president was George H.W. Bush, father of the current president George W. Bush, who is a Methodist.

Six of the presidents have been Presbyterian. Woodrow Wilson, the son of a Presbyterian minister, served as president of the College of New Jersey. Two members of the (Dutch) Reformed Church in America (Martin Van Buren and Theodore Roosevelt) and one Congregationalist (Calvin Coolidge) have served as president. That so many members of the older Protestant churches have been elected to lead the country reflects the high educational level and wealth concentrated among their members.

While Congressional membership more closely parallels America's religious profile, with the largest number being drawn from the Catholic, Baptist, and United Methodist Churches, again the Episcopalians and Presbyterians are over-represented, considering their relatively small membership percentages in the population, and there are a healthy number of Congregationalists (from the United Church of Christ). Among the prominent mainline Protestants holding leadership positions in the Senate are Episcopalians Phil Gramm, Charles Robb, and John Warner; Lutheran Ernest F. Hollings; Congregationalist Bob Kerrey; and Presbyterian John D. Rockefeller IV. In the House of Representatives, Presbyterian Dick Armey is the House Majority Leader.

The Protestant churches are also well represented in the governor's mansions across the United States, including such notables as Presbyterian Christie Todd Whitman (former governor of New Jersey), Episcopalian Mike Foster (Louisiana), and Lutheran Gary Johnson (New Mexico).

Dealing with Politics—How the Churches Operate

Through the 19th century, the churches frequently voiced their positions on matters affecting national and local public policy. Scanning the records of the churches' governing bodies, one comes across numerous resolutions, petitions to Congress, and open letters to prominent politicians from the president on down. These documents attempt to call the attention of political leaders to moral issues involved in pieces of legislation before them or to needs of the people, that the churches believed legislators should address. Working both formally and informally, church leaders have exerted great influence in both promoting and blocking proposed legislation.

With the fracturing of the Protestant community (there are more than 1,000 Christian denominations in America today), churches saw the effectiveness of presenting a united voice to legislatures, and they found a role for leaders who could not only speak for their own church but for all Protestant churches. Thus, in the late 19th century, the larger Protestant bodies began to entertain proposals for a Protestant cooperative council.

In 1908, 33 denominations came together to constitute the Federal Council of Churches. Among its first actions was appointing a Commission on Church and Social Service, and in 1912 it adopted the "Social Creed of the Churches," a lengthy document addressing a number of issues, especially those dividing labor and industry. The Council promoted the use of military chaplains during World War I and became deeply involved in peace efforts in the decades between the World Wars.

PROTESTANTS IN THE WHITE HOUSE

These are the religious affiliations of the presidents of the United States who were affiliated with mainline Protestant churches.

Episcopalian
George Washington, James Madison, James Monroe, William Henry Harrison, John Tyler, Zachary Taylor, Franklin Pierce, Chester A. Arthur, Franklin D. Roosevelt, Gerald Ford, Ronald Reagan, George H. W. Bush.

Presbyterian
Andrew Jackson, James Buchanan, Grover Cleveland, Benjamin Harrison, Woodrow Wilson, Dwight Eisenhower. (Note: James Polk was a Presbyterian but converted to the Methodist faith.)

Dutch Reformed
Martin Van Buren
Theodore Roosevelt

Congregationalist
Calvin Coolidge

In the 1920s and 1930s, many of the council's member churches were affected by the split between Fundamentalist and Modernist Christians. The Modernists advocated a variety of changes in the churches including a positive response to the new scientific and industrialized world that was coming into being. Fundamentalists believed that in making changes, the Modernists were moving away from their adherence to the essential and traditional affirmations of the Christian faith. As most of the larger churches came under the control of the more liberal Modernists in the 1930s, the Federal Council of Churches took on a decidedly Modernist outlook. Fundamentalists complained that the council placed too much emphasis on social and political issues and neglected the evangelistic task of winning people to Christ and nurturing believers in local churches.

The Federal Council, by including in its membership most of the larger Protestant churches (the Southern Baptist Convention being a major exception), began to develop many of the attributes of an "established" church for America. This perception was passed on to the National Council of Churches of Christ that superseded the Federal Council in 1950. The National Council also assumed additional status because of its relationship with an international network of Christian churches, the World Council of Churches. Most of the members of the National Council were also members of the World Council.

Through the National Council of Churches, based in New York City, the member churches have attempted to speak to their adherents, the public at large, and the powerful structures that run the society, especially political leaders. Extending the influence of the National Council are a set of 50 state councils, most based in each state's capital city, who can also speak to their constituencies and to state governments.

The National Council at Work Today

The role of the National Council has been twofold, a fact that has often brought confusion to the members and churches that support it. Most frequently, the members of the Council speak as a united voice to the public and to the government on matters of public policy. They attempt to present the opinion of either a consensus or a clear majority of the Council's members on important matters. At other times it assumes what is termed a "prophetic" role. Based upon the deliberation of the church representatives who make up its ruling authority, the Council speaks on

Gathering at the table

Nearly 300 delegates from 36 Protestant churches gathered at this 2001 meeting of the General Assembly of the National Council of Churches (NCC). This group helps the NCC set its national policies and priorities.

matters about which the churches may be conflicted and themselves debating. In these cases, it hopes to win the member churches to its position.

On a variety of occasions, the Council has been quite controversial in its positions on such issues as apartheid in South Africa, the Vietnam War, and the admission of the Peoples' Republic of China into the United Nations. As early as 1942, Evangelicals opposed to the perceived liberalism of the member churches of the Federal Council, formed an alternative organization, the National Association of Evangelicals, which continues to speak for more conservative Evangelical churches and conservative members of the larger Protestant churches.

Today the National Council includes 36 Protestant and Eastern Orthodox churches, including those older Protestant church bodies that have been the primary subject of this book—the Episcopal Church, the United Church of Christ, the Presbyterians Church (USA), the Evangelical Lutheran Church in America, and the Reformed Church in America. Also among the prominent Council members is the United Methodist Church, which has increasingly identified itself with the older Protestant churches.

Representatives of these churches meet annually in an assembly. The Council maintains an office in Washington, D.C., near Capitol

Hill, which houses its Public Witness and Legislative Advocacy program unit. This agency gathers and spreads information about ongoing legislation. It also lobbies on behalf of the Council and its member churches on a wide variety of issues.

The NCC has been most active in promoting integration and opposing racism; supporting pro-choice issues in the abortion debates; championing the rights of women in both the secular and church contexts; supporting the improvement of public education as opposed to government support for private alternatives; and working to end poverty.

Environmental Issues

At least since the era of the dust bowls in the 1930s (see the box at left), the Protestant community has shown its concern for environmental issues, and in the last generation has issued numerous statements on topics such as water pollution, global warming, and the destruction of the rain forests. Much of this consideration has grown out of the belief that the world was created by God and given to humanity as a trust to protect and use for the benefit of all. Many have spoken of the earth as sacred, though most Protestants draw back from any attempt to deify nature. However, all Protestants find the world to be awe-inspiring and affirm its goodness as the realm into which God brought Jesus Christ.

It should be noted that the broader environmental movement has been critical of a traditional Christian affirmation that God gave humanity "dominion" (control) over the earth and nature. They claim this affirmation has been misunderstood and actually has become a factor in the destruction of the environment.

In 1991, Protestant leaders sent an open letter to the American religious community signed by 32 prominent scientists, all Nobel Prize winners. The letter called attention to the perceived poor public response to environmental dangers, most caused by the spread of the industrial society. The letter prompted conversations between Protestants and other religious leaders who agreed that one item lacking in the current public debate is a unified vision of the world and humanity's place within the larger web of life. The transformation of thought and behavior that such a vision might bring seemed to be the natural concern of the spiritual life.

Following the letter, religious leaders already concerned with environmental issues intensified their discussions and in 1993 gathered

THE DUST BOWLS

A terrible drought severely affected the midwestern United States in the early 1930s. Thousands of farmers were put out of business by the years without enough rain. Many were forced to leave their homes in states such as Oklahoma, Kansas, and Texas and head west to find work.

The drought was a significant economic disaster, especially for farmers who could not grow their crops. But the ecological devastation of years without rain also raised many issues of land and water management. The combination of personal tragedy and environmental damage caused many Protestant communities to pay more attention to ecological issues.

to found what became known as the National Religious Partnership for the Environment. The organization immediately shot to the forefront in the environmental movement by its gathering the support of important religious bodies representing Catholic, Jewish, Evangelical, and Protestant faiths. The most prominent and visible Protestant leader was Edmond Browning, then the Presiding Bishop of the Episcopal Church.

The partnership has been unique in its ability to mine the common elements of the Jewish and Christian heritages in developing a spiritual vision of an environmentally sound world. It has access to tens of thousands of local congregations through which local programs can be started on the wide variety of environmental concerns, ranging from recycling to pressuring Congress to approve global environmental treaties.

War and Peace

Issues of war and peace are among the most difficult that religious people face. While people of faith are overwhelmingly committed to the value of peace, the actual conflicts in which people and nations find themselves raise ethical questions that often do not yield to simple solutions. The desire for peace competes with the demands of justice and the calls of patriotism. In the Bible, Christians are confronted with stories of God's people engaging in war and the church has, through most of its history, sanctioned the actions of armies for a variety of causes and rarely denied governments the authority to wage war.

Increasingly, however, in the modern world, voices have challenged the traditional thinking on war and peace. They argue that Christianity clearly sets individuals on the side of peace and that Christians should withdraw their support from all violence, especially warfare. Through the 20th century, this position has been strengthened by the availability of weapons that can wipe out all human life, thus making the renunciation of war all the more imperative.

Pacifism means refusing to participate in killing of any kind. This philosophy came forward at the time of the Protestant Reformation when a number of smaller groups, the so-called radical reform churches, made pacifism a part of their protest of the state church. From these early groups developed what are referred to today as the Peace Churches—Quakers, Mennonites, and Brethren (of several kinds).

Most Protestants have, however, followed the early reformers in articulating a doctrine of just war, the idea that under certain circumstances, Christians may and even should engage in war. This doctrine was frequently cited by religious leaders who supported America's entrance into World Wars I and II.

The Fellowship of Reconciliation (FOR), founded in England in 1914 several months after the beginning of World War I, represented the spread of pacifism into mainline Protestantism. It grew out of the relationship of British Quaker Henry Hodgkin (1988–1933) and a German Lutheran, Friedrich Siegmund-Schultze (1885–1969). A chaplain to Kaiser Wilhelm, Siegmund-Schultze was arrested more than 25 times for anti-war activities between 1914 and 1917, and was one of the first people exiled from Germany when the Nazis came to power.

The American chapter of the Fellowship was founded in 1915 and included among its early members Presbyterian Norman Thomas (1994–1968) and Episcopalian Paul Jones (1880–1941), a former bishop of Utah who had been removed from office because of his peace advocacy. Much of their wartime activity focused on providing support for conscientious objectors (called "COs," see the box at left) from mainline churches.

Another Episcopalian, John Nevin Sayre (1885–1982), drew on his acquaintance with President Woodrow Wilson to help stop the inhumane treatment of COs who had been arrested for refusing the draft.

After the war, the FOR moved into other issues, including the support of labor union organizing. However, during World War I, called the "war to end all wars," the fellowship enjoyed an era of some success as many Protestant ministers identified themselves as pacifists.

FOR faced a significant challenge following the Japanese attack on Pearl Harbor in 1941, when many of its supporters gave up their pacifism. At the same time, however, many stuck to their commitments, in spite of the pro-war atmosphere that dominated the country and the larger denominations. FOR leaders protested the movement of Japanese Americans into internment camps in 1942 and opposed saturation bombing of military and civilian targets inside Germany by United States-led Allied forces. After the war, they opposed the adoption of universal military training that would have sent all of America's male youth into the Armed Forces for at least a year, followed by additional years in the reserves.

A WAY OUT OF WAR

A conscientious objector (CO) is a person who believes that it is wrong to kill another human being in war. The military defines conscientious objection as a "firm, fixed, and sincere objection to war in any form or the bearing of arms" because of deeply-held moral, ethical, or religious beliefs. In some cases, COs can serve in non-combat roles such as medical divisions.

Reformed Church minister A. J. Muste (1885–1967) was among the prominent leaders who emerged in the years after World War II in which the organization's attention was refocused on the atomic threat. The anti-nuclear focus later developed into FOR's criticism of the Vietnam War. The group found unexpected additional support when many church leaders who were not pacifists suggested that the Vietnam War did not meet the criteria of a just war.

Through the Vietnam War and in the decades since, FOR has been present almost everywhere violence has erupted to work for peaceful solutions to global conflict. Much of its work has been within the churches and with organizations such as the National and World Councils of Churches, where pacifism is a distinct minority opinion. Among its recent programs have been efforts to look again at the nations of the former Soviet Union. As the Soviet Union became Russia and other nations beginning in the early 1990s, regional conflicts arose between some of the new states and FOR rallied against those conflicts. FOR has gained its widest audience in its work with the victims of war. For example, after the Bosnian war of the 1990s, it brought students from Bosnia to the United States for a chance to study and rebuild their lives.

Begun as a Protestant Christian organization based on the radical love ethic of Jesus, the organization has become much more of an interfaith organization in the last generation and has incorporated the active nonviolent stance most identified with Mahatma Gandhi and Martin Luther King, Jr. It has drawn Jews, Muslims, Hindus, and Buddhists into its international membership and has incorporated the pacifist teachings of each tradition into its thinking.

In the months after the attacks on the United States on September 11, 2001, when New York and Washington, D.C., were attacked by terrorists, it has found itself searching for new ways to express its commitment to peace and justice through nonviolence. Those efforts include programs to prevent the spread of war to Iraq and the need to build a permanent peaceful solution to the conflict between Israel and the Palestinians.

Faith-Based Initiatives

As the 21st century begins, Protestant churches have become involved with government programs that provide money for religious groups to deliver social services. It has long been the case that religious agencies,

WHAT IS A "JUST WAR"?
In the phrase "just war," just means fair or in the spirit of justice. Most Western Christians understand a "just war" as being a conflict that is in response to direct aggression, such response being proportional to the attack. It speaks against civilian casualties and calls for any action to be one that permanently ends further aggression. Most Protestants will cite the idea of a "just war" in those cases where they offer to support a war effort.

most notably Catholic Charities and Lutheran Social Services, use government money to develop large community assistance programs. To accomplish this task, the churches were required to establish a separate non-profit corporation that could receive the government funds. These non-profit organizations had to abide by a number of government regulations. For example, they had to deliver services without discriminating against people based on their religions.

The new program announced by President George W. Bush in 2001 is aimed at allowing church groups to apply for government money to provide social services otherwise federally mandated (such as distributing food to the poor) without the time-consuming and often burdensome process of creating a new corporation and abiding by federal guidelines. It is the assumption of the new faith-based initiative program that religious groups are better able to provide these services than government agencies.

The proposal, which came to the fore during Bush's campaign for the presidency, has sparked a broad debate within the Protestant churches. There is widespread agreement that religious groups will deliver, along with services, a touch of love and caring for the individuals being served. For example, there is a desire to meet the immediate physical needs of the poor, but there is also a desire to communicate to them a message of self-worth, a hope for a better life, and means to achieve that better life.

However, it is in communicating that message that many find a problem. Can one communicate a sense of self-worth or hope without communicating the religious faith as well, in this case the Protestant Christian faith? Some have argued that it is very difficult at best and almost impossible in practice. As such, to allow churches to deliver government mandated services will invariably involve both undue government entanglement in religion and the government's sponsorship of those religions that receive funds.

The Protestant community has been split, with prominent leadership on both sides. Those who have had experiences with Catholic Charities and Lutheran Social Services have tended to affirm the greater good that can come by freeing the churches to do even more good. Those most concerned with issues of keeping church and state apart tend to highlight the potential danger in the churches becoming dependent on state funds. Faith-based initiatives are most likely to be the issue around which new perspectives on church-state relations will develop in the decades ahead.

Protestant Politics

Protestants approach the political process somewhat differently from other religious groups in America. They have an image of themselves as the mainstream of American religious life. Unlike other groups, they do not see themselves as having to justify their entrance into political deliberations, and they do not celebrate accomplishments when they are given a voice in the political process. Protestants were here when the nation was founded, and they see themselves as an integral part of the total American culture and political process.

They do bemoan the fact that many government officials seem to ignore them in favor of expediency and narrow political interests, and neglect the higher moral values the churches represent. However, Protestants continue to believe it is their responsibility to raise the moral issues and assume the rightness of their significant presence in Washington and the state capitals.

6

Important American Protestant Leaders

TO A LARGE EXTENT, AMERICAN LEADERSHIP AND PROTESTANT leadership in America has been synonymous. Protestants have been outstanding in every area of American life—social, cultural, political, and economic. In this chapter we have tried to highlight a very few who are typical of the many who have made significant contributions to the national life.

John Winthrop (1588–1649)

John Winthrop was a young British lawyer with a promising career ahead of him. However, because of his commitment to the Reformed Protestant faith, he decided to throw his lot in with the Puritans who later settled Massachusetts. His intellectual achievements were recognized by his fellow believers, who elected him as their first governor. His career would, however, be a stormy one. A staunch Calvinist, he believed in a limited democracy—limited to those few allowed to exercise the vote (male church members in good standing) and limited in scope (granting to the elected officials such as himself almost dictatorial powers).

His heavy-handed tactics got him in trouble more than once and on three occasions he was removed from office, the last time being followed by a trial for acting above and outside his office. Each time, however, his

Man in the middle
John Winthrop, an English minister, was governor of the British colony at Plymouth and an important chronicler of life in early America.

PRECEDING PAGE
Presbyterian from Princeton
Woodrow Wilson brought his strong Protestant beliefs to his work as president.

replacement proved unsuitable, and the voters returned him to the governor's chair. His last term was from 1646 until his death three years later. Not a man to be trifled with, he is remembered as the authority who ordered the banishment of the colony's two famous dissenters, Anne Hutchinson (see page 28) and Roger Williams, who later founded Rhode Island.

His political career would have been enough to secure his place in the history books, but he also was among the first generation of Puritans who left extensive written records. His journal, later published as *The History of New England from 1630 to 1649*, remains one of the key sources for understanding the history of the pioneering settlement around Boston. Also, on the trip from Great Britain aboard the *Arbella*, Winthrop preached a famous sermon, "A Model of Christian Charity," which became a summary of the Puritan's purpose in the new world. He called upon his fellow church members to remember that "the care of the public must oversway all private respects by which not only conscience but mere civil policy doth bind us." He also said that based on their covenant with God they had a God-given commission to rule themselves. This document would later be cited as the root of the idea of a "moral purpose" in America's understanding of itself.

George Whitefield (1714–1770)

George Whitefield was not an American, but during his several trips through the British colonies he was instrumental in the transformation of the separate colonial centers into a single nation. He was 19 years old when he entered Pembroke College at Oxford University, where he met John Wesley (the founder of Methodism). His association with this devout fellow student changed both their lives. As he was about to leave for America, he altered Wesley's career by calling him to take over the work in Bristol, England (which would become a prominent Methodist center).

Whitefield had made a brief trip to America in 1738, but upon his return to England found no place in a British pulpit. Therefore, he began to preach out-of-doors to all who would listen. He found an especially attentive following in the coalfields near Bristol, and preached to the miners after their daily shifts. When he returned to America, he traveled from city to city along the Atlantic coast, preaching to large crowds who flocked to hear a man who was perhaps the greatest orator of the period. His preaching services became the first truly universal cultural experience shared by the Americans—whether they were Anglicans, Congregationalists, Baptists, or nonreligious. Using Whitefield's words and ideas, ministers of every denomination had something in common to talk about.

Whitefield not only affected the colonists, but they changed him. He was a devout member of the Church of England. However, while visiting with his Congregationalist colleagues in the colonies, he accepted a Calvinist point of view. The major issue over which Anglican (and Methodists) and Calvinists parted company was predestination. Calvinists concluded that God must have predestined those who would ultimately accept Christ and be saved. In contrast, Anglicans generally believed that there was an element of free choice of God's grace by the believer.

Whitefield later broke with John Wesley and became associated with a small Calvinist body sponsored by the Countess of Huntington that combined revivalism with Calvinist theology, and was later absorbed into Presbyterianism.

In all, Whitefield made seven trips to America. He preached his last sermon on Exeter Green in New Hampshire. He closed by telling his audience, "I shall soon be in a world where time, age, pain, and

FAMOUS AMERICAN EPISCOPALIANS

Edwin "Buzz" Aldrin (b.1930), astronaut

Washington Irving (1783–1859), author

Robert E. Lee (1807–1870), Civil War general

Fr. Clement Moore (1779–1863), wrote the poem "The Night Before Christmas"

Colin Powell (b.1937), secretary of state

Vincent Price (1911–1993), actor

Sammy Sosa, (b. 1968) baseball player

sorrow are unknown. My body fails, my spirit expands." He passed away early the next morning. Collection of his sermons, many of which were preached numerous times to different audiences as he toured the countryside, have been published in many editions. The first was in 1771 and others have been as recent at 1990 (*Select Sermons of George Whitefield With an Account of His Life*, by J.C. Ryle). They are also collected on the Internet. They remain as a record of the message he bequeathed to an emerging nation.

Samuel Provoost (1742–1815)

Samuel Provoost grew up during the years that George Whitefield was touring America. Provoost was among the members of the first graduating class at New York's Columbia University (then called King's College); he later continued his studies at Cambridge University in England. Ordained in England (there being no bishop to ordain him in America), Provoost returned to New York to become the assistant pastor of Trinity Church.

All was well for several years, but by 1769, Provoost had emerged as the most outspoken pro-Revolutionary minister among the Anglicans in New York and was forced to resign. He lived in retirement for several years, but once hostilities broke out, he fought in the Patriot army. Thus, when the Revolution was successful, he was among the few Anglican clergy who had cast his lot with the former colonists and was welcomed back into parish life in New York. He assumed a critical role as chaplain to the Continental Congress and then in the construction of the Episcopal Church, which replaced the Church of England as the Anglican body in the new nation. He was a major force in that church's inclusion of a democratic process in its structure. In 1787, he traveled to England where he was consecrated as one of the three bishops for the church.

William White, consecrated at the same time as Provoost, became the presiding bishop of the Episcopal Church, but Provoost had his own place in the spotlight once the national government shifted its center from Philadelphia to New York. Provoost became the first chaplain to the newly organized United States Senate. His role in reminding the nation's leaders of their religious roots was punctuated by his being chosen to preside at the memorial service following President George Washington's death in 1799.

FAMOUS AMERICAN LUTHERANS

Troy Aikman (b.1966), pro football player

David Hasselhoff (b.1952), actor

Lou Holtz (b.1937), college football coach

Al Kaline (b.1934), baseball player

Tom Landry (b.1924), pro football coach

Norman Schwarzkopf (b.1934), Gulf War general

Sally Struthers (b.1948), actress

Bruce Willis (b.1955) actor

A pioneering poet
Phillis Wheatley (c.1753–1784) became one of the first African Americans to achieve any sort of artistic fame as a popular poet and writer. Thirty-nine of her poems were published in 1773 as Poems on Various Subjects, Religious and Moral, *her only work. This illustration comes from a later edition of that book.*

Phillis Wheatley (1753–1784)

One can hardly imagine being snatched from one's parents as a child of seven and being transported across an ocean on a sailing ship, only to land in a foreign world where a totally new life and identity awaited. But this is what happen to a Senegalese girl in 1761. Up arriving in Boston, she was purchased as a slave by a couple, John and Susannah Wheatley, and given the new name Phillis. A frail child, she was trained as a maid. However, she was also given a basic education, and while still in her childhood learned not only to speak English, but to read and write it. She went on to study Latin.

The couple who owned her observed her linguistic abilities and kept her housekeeping duties light so she could have time every day to read. Part of her regular reading was the Bible, and when the Wheatleys were comfortable that she not only understood their faith but had become an adherent of it, they sponsored Phillis as a member of their congregation, the famous Old South Church. She was baptized in 1771, the first African American to join the Congregational church.

The Wheatleys had come to understand that they had an unusual teenager. She had moved from learning to read and write to demonstrating her mastery of English in her own literary work. Her first published work was a eulogy written on the occasion of the death of the

To the King's Most Excellent Majesty

An excerpt from a 1768 poem by Phillis Wheatley.

*Your subjects hope, dread Sire, the crown upon your
    brows may flourish long,
And that your arm may in your God be strong.
Oh, may your sceptre num'rous nations sway,
And all with love and readiness obey.*

*But how shall we the British King reward?
Rule thou in peace, our father and our lord!
'Midst the remembrance of thy favors past,
The meanest peasants most admire the last.
May George, beloved by all nations round.
Live with heaven's choicest, constant blessings crowned.
Great God! direct and guard him on high,
And from his head let every evil fly;
And may each clime with equal gladness see
A monarch's smile can set his subjects free.*

famous minister George Whitefield. As other works were published (and she was the only female slave allowed to publish her writings while still a slave), the fact of her accomplishment challenged common assumptions about the supposedly limited ability of Africans.

The Wheatleys granted Phillis her freedom in 1773, and that same year she sailed for England, where she was received as a celebrity. Whitefield's sponsor, the Countess of Huntington, was among those who went out of their way to entertain her. While in London, Wheatley's only book, *Poems on Various Subjects, Religious and Moral*, was published.

Wheatley is celebrated today as a pious Christian, an outstanding poet, and a spokesperson for her people at a time when most were not allowed a voice. However, she spent the last years of her life in obscurity, working alone in a boarding house in a poorer section of Boston. Her accomplishments were forgotten until the 1830s when the abolitionists rediscovered her poems and brought them to the public as support for their arguments to end the institution of slavery.

Elijah Lovejoy (1802–1837)

Among the people who would have read the poems of Phillis Wheatley was Presbyterian minister and abolitionist Elijah Lovejoy. The son of a minister, as a child Lovejoy was given an education and a motivation to help rid the world of sin before the second coming of Christ.

After finishing college, he moved to the West to bring (so his teachers had told him) the civilization of the East to the emerging settlements. In 1826 he landed in St. Louis and started his own school. Though successful, he decided to give up teaching in 1830 to work for the local newspaper.

In 1832, Lovejoy had an intense religious experience, something he had been hoping for since his years in college. As a result, he finally decided to study theology and enter the ministry. He studied at Princeton for a year and was licensed to preach in 1833. Meanwhile, some acquaintances in St. Louis raised the money to purchase a printing press and set him in place as the editor of a new newspaper, the *St. Louis Observer*. His editorials came out in favor of temperance and against slavery, neither cause favored by the hard-drinking, slave-owning Missourians—even most Presbyterians.

During his years in St. Louis, Lovejoy became more and more radical on the issue of slavery and his rhetoric more and more harsh toward any who opposed what emerged as full-blown abolitionism, demanding the immediate end to the wicked institution of slavery. His support for the cause increased after 1836 when he moved his paper across the river to Alton, Illinois (then a free state). Soon after his arrival, he founded the Illinois Anti-Slavery Society.

His sermons and his editorials were increasingly unpopular, and on several occasions Lovejoy barely escaped from mobs intent upon expressing their anger at him personally—and painfully. Public anger was not lessened by editorials defending his right, granted in the Constitution, to hold and publish minority ideas.

To stop his publishing, the mobs in Alton destroyed his press on several occasions. The conflict came to a head in November 1837 when a mob attacked the heavily guarded warehouse where Lovejoy's latest press had been secured. In the shootout he was killed, and after the last

FAMOUS AMERICAN PRESBYTERIANS

Jane Addams (1860–1935), social reformer

Aaron Burr (1756–1836), U.S. vice president

John C. Calhoun (1782–1850), U.S. vice president

Katie Cannon (b.1950), African-American ethics scholar

John Foster Dulles (1888–1959), secretary of state

John Glenn (b. 1921), astronaut and senator

Jimmy Stewart (1908–1997), actor

of the defenders fled, the mob dismantled the press and threw it in the Mississippi River. Lovejoy died a martyr whose memory was resurrected when the cause he championed became the law of the land.

Margaret E. Sangster (1838–1912)

Protestants were not known as social radicals during the first two centuries of America's existence. They tended to identify with the social order, and while working to improve and reform it, people such as Elijah Lovejoy were exceptions. A more typical crusader was Margaret E. Sangster, who at a time in which women were still very much seen as having their proper place in the home, made her statement by her professional life. Her parents, the Munsons, were devout members of the Reformed Church in America, and like most families saw little need to give their female children much education. Margaret, much like Phyllis Wheatley, had a talent with words and as a teenager began to write professionally, her first published work appearing when she was just 17 years old.

She married at the age of 20, however, and put her writing aside to concentrate on family matters until her husband's death in 1871. She again picked up her pen and began a "second" career as a writer and editor. She became an editor for *Hearth and Home* magazine and set a new goal to make herself a role model for young Christian women.

She both wrote on the Christian life and demonstrated her perspective in her own life. She became editor of *Christian at Work* (1875), assistant editor of the *Christian Intelligencer* (1881), and then editor of *Harper's Bazaar* (1889), for which she is most well known. In the meantime, she had become a popular poet, wrote *Manual of Missions for the Reformed Church*, and edited a series of Sunday school books (popular Christian education material just coming into their own at the time). Her love of children led her to write several children's books, two of which, *Elizabeth, Age Nine* and *Are the Children at Home?*, became bestsellers.

Unlike her contemporaries Francis Willard and Carrie Chapman Catt, Sangster was not particularly a crusader for women. However, her accomplishments demonstrated the capabilities to which the women's movement could regularly point in making their case for women's equality.

The Beecher Family

Probably no family name was more associated with Protestant dominance in American public life than that of the Beechers. Henry Ward Beecher (1813–1887, above), for 40 years the pastor of Plymouth Congregational Church in Brooklyn, New York, was the most well-known clergyman in America in the late 19th century, in spite of challenges to his progressive theology and a major scandal involving a woman who was not his wife.

Beecher was the son of Lyman Beecher (1775–1863), who was ordained a Presbyterian but also pastored Congregational churches and opposed the end of the state-supported church in Connecticut in 1817. Through the 1820s he staunchly defended traditional doctrine against Unitarians who denied the Trinity, and in 1835 he himself faced charges of heresy—although he was cleared by his fellow Presbyterians.

Henry Ward was not Lyman's only outstanding offspring. His daughter, writing under married name of Harriet Beecher Stowe (1811–1896), wrote the novel *Uncle Tom's Cabin*. The novel sold half a million copies during the 1850s and is regarded as the most influential text in mobilizing anti-slavery sentiment in the northern states prior to the Civil War. After the war she became the editor of a popular women's periodical, *Hearth and Home*.

Henry Ward Beecher came into his own just as the new scientific findings in geology and biology were shaking the foundations of traditional Christian thought. He was a pioneer spokesperson for what would in the next century become known as Modernism. He argued that theories of evolution from one species to another could be reconciled with the Bible. Under threat of a heresy trial, he withdrew from the Congregational denomination and continued as pastor of an independent congregation. He was an able and articulate spokesperson for the new theology that came to dominate most of the larger Protestant churches in the next century.

Woodrow Wilson (1856–1924)

While the majority of the American presidents have been Protestants, few have been so identified with their church as was Woodrow Wilson (1856-1924). The son of a Southern Presbyterian minister, Wilson graduated from Princeton, became a lawyer, and eventually finished a Ph.D. in political science. He moved to New Jersey and became a professor and then president of Princeton. His widely publicized actions to modernize the school led to an offer by the Democratic Party to run for governor of New Jersey. The governor's chair proved the springboard for his nomination to the presidency. When, in 1912, the Republican Party split into two camps, Wilson was elected president.

Wilson's Christian values had already been shown in his fights for political reform in New Jersey. As president, he supported the labor union movement's attempts to establish itself, opposed excessive corporate influence in Washington, and helped created the Federal Reserve, the national system for regulating money and the banks. Wilson, committed to peace, kept America out of World War I until the sinking of the passenger ship *Lusitania* by German forces in 1917 made it impossible to oppose national sentiment. However, after the war Wilson championed a peace that was aimed at preventing another such war, including the establishment of a League of Nations. While such a League was created, it was a weak organization, made even weaker by America not joining it. Wilson was largely taken out of the picture by a stroke that hit him while promoting the League around the country. His vision of the League would finally be realized in the United Nations.

William Jennings Bryan (1860–1925)

For more than half a century, beginning with the publication of Charles Darwin's *The Descent of Man* in 1871, the Protestant churches became the battleground on which conservative Christians, tied to belief in the literal truth of the Bible, fought with Modernists over the way the Bible should be read. Few ideas have so challenged such literal readings (including the idea of a special creation of humans in the Garden of Eden some 6,000 to 10,000 years ago) as the idea of evolution.

According to Darwin's theory, the evolution of animals led to the appearance of humans and this process took millions of years. Conservatives, eventually called Fundamentalists (for their allegiance to what they saw as the Fundamentals of the faith), attempted to stem the tide of Modernist thought with a variety of methods, including court cases.

The Fundamentalist controversy climaxed in the 1920s, and through the first decades of the century it found a champion in William Jennings Bryan (1860–1925), as great an orator in his day as was Henry Ward Beecher in the previous generation (see page 107). A lawyer, Bryan made his early mark in politics. Elected to Congress in 1890, he went on to become the Democratic Party's candidate for president on three occasions (1896, 1900, 1908). He eventually served as secretary of state (1913–1915) under Wilson.

However, he resigned from Wilson's cabinet over his disagreements with his fellow Presbyterian's foreign policies. After his national political career ended, Bryan became a nationwide campaigner for peace and temperance, both causes rooted in his conservative Protestant faith.

A national figure
William Jennings Bryan was one of the most important and well-known personalities of the early 20th century. A powerful and fiery speaker, he took his case for Fundamentalism from the halls of politics to the pulpits of churches.

In the meantime, Tennessee passed a law against teaching the theory of evolution in the public schools, and in 1925 Bryan agreed to prosecute the test case against high school teacher John Scopes. The Scopes trial became famous because of the confrontation of Bryan with his agnostic (not believing in any supreme being) opponent, lawyer Clarence Darrow. Bryan won the trial but was widely perceived to have lost the intellectual exchange. He died a few days after the trial concluded, his death signaling to many the end of an era. Within a few years power in the Presbyterian Church had shifted toward the Modernist perspective, evident in a series of actions relative to control of the seminaries, the ordination of ministers, and the appointment of missionaries.

Bishop Carol Jay Gallagher (b. 1955)

The larger Protestant churches have been beset on one side by conservative movements and churches who saw the changes in Protestantism as an abandonment of the tradition. On the other side, the more progressive groups have caught the waves of the future and seemingly left the Protestants standing still. For example, through the early 20th century, Protestant leaders marshaled all of the arguments against female clergy that had begun to manifest in the more Evangelical churches. By the middle of the 20th century, however, the leadership noticeably shifted and one by one women were admitted both to the ordained ministry and the highest national church leadership posts in all the mainline Protestant churches. The half-century of change mirrored a variety of attitude changes about the place of racial and ethnic minorities in society, the emergence of cultural pluralism, and the shortcoming of the churches in dealing with both.

The changing attitude of the late-20th century has been no better summarized than in the career of Carol Jay Gallagher. Her father was a Presbyterian minister. Her mother, Betty Walking Stick Theobald was the product of a Cherokee Christian family. Her great-great-great-grandmother was among those Cherokee who were forced from their home in North Carolina to a reservation in Oklahoma in the 1830s.

Following seminary training, Gallagher was ordained to the Episcopal priesthood in 1991, two years after African-American Barbara Harris had become the first female bishop in the Episcopal Church. Gallagher served churches in the Diocese of Delaware, most recently at

St. Anne's Church in Middletown, and became the mother of three children.

Gallagher's election and consecration as a bishop on April 6, 2002, marked the culmination of a very different and less heralded trend in Protestant thought, the discarding of the paternalism that has been a hallmark of the church's attitude as Christianity permeated Native American life. Quietly through the decades since World War II, church leaders began to recognize the legitimacy and then the positive contributions possible from Native American culture.

As a bishop, Gallagher has addressed the spirituality of Native American people as she speaks about Christianity. She emphasizes the importance Native people ascribe to keeping a close connection to one's immediate family and one's people. As suffragan bishop (an assistant or subordinate bishop of a diocese) of southern Virginia, her primary duties are now centered on pastoral care for clergy families and assisting the smaller congregations in the diocese. Along with her job, Gallagher is completing a Ph.D. in urban affairs, and serves on the national church's Council of Indian Ministries and the anti-racism committee.

Protestant Americans

Any number of Protestant leaders have represented the Protestant community equally well and could have been selected for inclusion here. Intellectual leaders from Timothy Dwight to Richard Niebuhr, social activists from Alexander Crummel to Carter Hayward, and great orators from Phillips Brooks to Peter Marshall are good examples.

The people of this faith group have dominated the American culture, for good and sometimes for ill. At their best, however, they have represented the ideals to which the majority of Americans have been committed and have nurtured leaders who, by forcing the dialogue between faith and culture, have, generation by generation, helped prepare the nation for its next moves forward.

7

Protestantism's Prospects in the New Century

PROTESTANTISM BEGINS THE NEW CENTURY WITH A RICH HERITAGE that has produced a large community of faith and continues to make a significant cultural impact. It faces an open future with many choices, the knowledge that weathering the changes of a turbulent century has given it, and vast resources of material wealth and talented leadership. Much of the future these churches will create will depend upon continuing longtime trends.

Signs of Decline

Several of the Protestant churches remain among the largest religious organizations (in numbers of members) in the United States. These include the Evangelical Lutheran Church in America(with more than 5 million members, the Presbyterian Church (USA) with some 3.5 million members, and the Lutheran Church Missouri Synod with 2.5 million members. The Episcopal Church reports 1.7 million and the United Church of Christ (the continuing Congregationalists) about 1.3 million.

At the beginning of the 19th century, the Congregationalists and the Episcopalians were the largest churches in the United States. However, they soon fell behind the rapidly growing Baptist, Methodist, and Roman Catholic churches. Through the 19th and 20th centuries, the several Protestant churches grew, and grew significantly, but did so in a country that was growing even faster. So while Protestant churches increased in membership, their size relative to the country's population as a whole slowly and steadily decreased. As the American public became more and more religious (as indicated by church membership), these churches remained among the larger national bodies, but also faced ever-increasing competition from other movements. Today, there are more than 1,000 different Protestant denominations, ranging from small groups of a few congregations to more than 50 with at least 1 million members (such as the African Methodist Episcopal Church, the Orthodox Church in America, and the Assemblies of God).

However, in spite of some signs of decline, the larger Protestant churches remain in the forefront of the American religious community. Still among the larger religious bodies in the country, their role is highlighted because of their willingness to assume some responsibility for the society and culture as a whole. That sense of responsibility leads them to insert themselves in the ongoing debate about everything from American foreign policy to the ethics of business leadership.

Protestantism has been notable within the American Christian community for its commitment to intellectual leadership and a trained clergy. The demand for a professionally qualified clergy has often been challenged. Critics charge that the emphasis on church leadership leads to a decline in genuine spirituality. Protestant leaders have responded that the two central points of the religious life—theological study and personal faith—have never been mutually exclusive. Their continuing large membership indicates that the attempt to balance the demands of both parts of faith have worked for many.

These two emphases have also dictated the churches' response to some of the larger trends in the last two centuries, especially the world missions movement and the ecumenical movement, which is the movement toward unifying the many strands of Christianity.

Global Commitments

Early in the 19th century, Protestant churches, most notably the Congregationalists and Presbyterians, began to put a substantial part of their resources into world missions. India, Africa, and China initially received Protestant missionaries and through the first half of the 20th century, missions were established in almost every area of the world.

This movement accompanied the attempt of different European countries to establish global empires. By the 1930s, most of the larger churches supported multi-national missionary enterprises.

The Protestant churches were radically changed by World War II. Lutherans, especially, were affected. Germany was their place of origin, and many Americans had extended family in Germany and the surrounding nations most devastated by the final attempts to crush the Nazi strongholds. Following the war, Lutherans internationally organized to rebuild Europe. Other churches made similar efforts to return Europe to its prewar state as soon as possible.

At the same time, the American churches found themselves deeply involved in the postwar changes around the world, possibly the most important being the dismantling of the colonial system that peaked in the 1960s. Plans to turn over mission churches to local leaders and to help them change into self-governing churches were speeded up. For Protestants, such plans included upgrading schools for ministers, plans for financial support to churches in poorer countries, and transferring American missionaries to positions under local control.

Back home, the change was accompanied by a dramatic re-education of church members who had for generations focused on donating money to support the spread of Christianity abroad. They now had to face the fact that their task was somewhat completed. In most countries of the world, an autonomous local affiliate had been created and it had assumed the task of spreading Christianity in its own area. American churches now assumed a partnership arrangement with these affiliated churches to assist them in their evangelical task.

At the same time, the widely-held belief in European and American cultural, and even racial, superiority died out. The belief had frequently blurred the mission of spreading Christianity. Thus it is not surprising to find that the transformation of the missionary enterprise around the world occurred concurrently with the Civil Rights movement in the United States. Much of the future of Protestantism is now tied to how it maintains its continuing global commitments.

Ecumenism

Through the 19th century, the Protestant movement in North America splintered into hundreds of competing denominations. That splintering continued through the 20th century. The competition between churches for members was also carried to the mission field where Lutherans and Presbyterians tried to gain members from Methodists and Baptists, and had to explain to non-Western people why the distinction between Episcopalians and Congregationalists was important. By the end of the 19th century, many missionaries concluded that denominational quarrels were a major obstacle to the missionary enterprise.

Consequently, missionaries issued the first important calls for the churches to find some way of minimizing, if not ending, the unfruitful competition. Initial efforts were made even in the early 19th century to assign different territories in the mission field to different churches. As early as 1846, British missionaries took the lead in founding an international Evangelical Alliance, and even earlier, some American Protestants had founded the Society for the Promotion of Christian Unity (1939). By the end of the 19th century, such calls had resulted in the formation of the ecumenical movement, its name coming from an old Greek word for household. Leaders asked how the different churches could become a better expression of the one household of God.

Internationally, the ecumenical movement culminated in 1948 with the formation of the World Council of Churches, in which a number of American denominations participated. Nationally, a number of the larger churches came together in the Federal Council of Churches in 1906, and the Council became the catalyst for the founding of a host of national and regional cooperative bodies. The Federal Council was superseded by the National Council of Churches of Christ in the U.S.A, in 1950.

The Federal and later the National Council had a profound effect on the larger Protestant bodies as it encouraged the different denominational families to come together. The Lutherans, for example, had been divided into more that 100 separate denominational bodies through the 19th century as Lutherans from different countries moved to America. However, by the end of World War I, most of these churches had dropped their use of Norwegian and Swedish and German languages, and the reasons for continued separation seemed far less important. Through a series of mergers the majority of the Lutheran synods (organizations) came together in 1988 as the Evangelical Lutheran Church in America.

Presbyterians had been primarily affected by disagreements over revivalism and then the Civil War. As the 20th century began, there were three large Presbyterian bodies. These eventually came together as the Presbyterian Church (USA) in 1983.

ANOTHER NEW CHURCH

Among the most interesting unions representative of the ecumenical endeavor was the 1957 merger that produced the United Church of Christ. This merger brought together German Americans with a Reformed and Lutheran background and British Americans out of the Puritan Congregationalist heritage.

As the new century begins, the interest in merging denominations that so marked American Protestantism in the decades since World War II appears to have died. The ecumenical contacts of the period have had a marked effect on tempering denominational competition and have produced a spirit of cooperation between the larger Protestant bodies. Many feel that further mergers, leading to the creation of a single large Protestant church, are unnecessary. They have redirected efforts toward cooperative activities in providing social services to the nation and speaking with a united voice on matters of general public and Christian interest.

Continuing Liberal/Conservative Protestant Issues

The longstanding and larger Protestant bodies are identified today with what is termed liberal Protestantism (along with other churches such as the United Methodist Church and the American Baptist churches in the United States). They continue the Modernist element from the Fundamentalist/Modernist controversy early in the 20th century (see page 48). In their efforts to remain loyal to the Protestant Christian heritage, they have decided that the heritage must always be in dialogue with the contemporary world and the most progressive elements of the intellectual establishment.

Liberal Protestants have, for example, been in the forefront of using modern academic historical techniques in their attempt to interpret the Bible. Liberal Protestants generally see the Bible as having been created by a complex process of assembling and editing ancient texts into the current narrative. They tend to view the Bible as an authoritative and inspired moral, spiritual, and religious text, while at the same time affirming it as the product of human endeavor, written by people deeply involved in their own historical situations.

Liberal Protestants have also been deeply affected by the new world opened by scientific inquiry and technological advances. A crucial battle was fought over the insights of biologists concerning the evolution of the animal world. Since the 1920s, liberal Protestants have attempted to develop theological perspectives that pay attention to scientific knowledge and are open to new scientific discoveries. At the same time, they confront the moral challenges presented by humankind's abilities to control an increasing number of elements of the physical world.

Coming together
Protestants join with many other faiths in times of crisis. Interfaith ceremonies such as this one held in Connecticut following the terrorist attacks of September 11, 2001, point to the continuing important role of faith in the life of America and the world.

In its attempt to be open to the changing world, liberal Protestants face a dilemma. On the one hand, they are involved with the most radical of ideas present in the culture. On the other, liberals face the charge by more conservative members that they are abandoning the tradition and the truths of the faith. The tension between being true to the tradition and discerning where the future is leading has meant that liberal Protestants have lost members who through the last century have come to feel that the churches have strayed too far from tradition. As a result, a set of conservative denominations have arisen that on one level mirror the larger Protestant bodies, but have adopted a more literal understanding of the Bible and Protestant faith statements, coupled with a more critical attitude toward science.

Included among these more conservative churches are the Presbyterian Church in America (formed by churches that rejected the merger that produced the Presbyterian Church [USA]); the Lutheran Church-Missouri Synod (which did not participate in the mergers leading to the formation of the Evangelical Lutheran Church in America); and the Christian Reformed Church (that shares the Dutch Reformed heritage). Following the acceptance of women in the priesthood, the Episcopal Church has experienced schisms (divisions) and the establishment of several new denominations that have adopted a conservative Anglican stance, the largest being the Anglican Catholic Church.

It is difficult to predict how these newer churches will do in the diverse American religious landscape in the next generation. In the short run they have been a haven for some who no longer feel at home in the church of their childhood.

During the 1990s, the issue of ordaining women was largely replaced as the most controversial issue by the issues of abortion and homosexuality. Liberal Protestants have tended to lean toward free choice on the abortion question and have conducted a generation-long debate on homosexuality, though only the United Church of Christ has allowed practicing homosexuals to be ordained. The more conservative churches have leaned toward the pro-life side of the abortion question and have been staunchly against allowing homosexuals into any church leadership positions.

Into the Future

In spite of the internal controversies that have disturbed the churches, the still-vital role of Protestant leadership in American life was demonstrated following the bombing of the Pentagon and World Trade Center on September 11, 2001. As the nation grieved, Protestant leaders were in the forefront of the response. Their words of inspiration and hope to the grieving were broadcast on the nation's airwaves, and they were prominently present in the varied ecumenical and interfaith services. The public listened to their call for understanding toward American Muslims and responded to their request not to take out their emotions on their Muslim neighbors.

Across the liberal-conservative spectrum, the various churches have brought their resources to bear on the resulting debates over the bombing and the further terrorist threat both at home and abroad. For the time being, the Protestant place at the heart of American life seems secure.

GLOSSARY

baptism the primary act of entrance into the Christian community. Most Protestant churches baptize infants by sprinkling or pouring a small quantity of water on their heads. Baptisms are usually held as part of Sunday worship services.

catechism a set of questions and answers concerning Christian beliefs and behavior. Protestant churches have adopted various catechisms as part of their official statements of doctrine. In past centuries, it was common for youth to be required to memorize all or part of the official catechism.

deist one who adopts the position that while God created the world, He does not have a continuing relationship with it. Deists believe since God does not interfere with the world, prayers are of no significance and miracles are impossible.

diocese a territory over which a bishop presides. Each diocese will contain a number of parishes (local churches).

communion one name commonly given in Protestant circles to the sacrament in which bread and wine are consumed as representations of the body and blood of Christ. The term emphasizes the unity of Christians that the sacrament symbolizes.

consubstantiation the particular view of the communion sacrament adopted by Martin Luther. Luther understood Christ to be present everywhere, but was particularly available to Christians in the form of the bread and wine at a communion service.

covenant an agreement that involves a promise by both parties to act in certain ways. God, it is believed, made a covenant with Abraham and his descendants, with the Jewish people when they received the Ten Commandments, and with all of humanity in Christ. Many Protestant groups have organized their churches based on a covenant.

ecumenical literally "household," it refers to the whole community of Christian believers. Ecumenical is a term used today to talk about relations between different Christian churches as they begin to recognize one another as fellow Christians.

elder a leader in the Christian church. The term may refer either to an ordained minister (a teaching elder in the Presbyterian church) or a lay person (a ruling elder in the Presbyterian system).

Eucharist the basic act of worship in Christianity, during which Christians consume bread and wine in remembrance of Jesus' last meal with his 12 Disciples. Most Protestant Christians believe that Christ is in some manner present to the believer through the Eucharist.

evangelize the mandate to Christians to tell the world about Jesus and his message.

grace God's favor to all people. Protestants teach that God's grace is freely given to all and not based upon anyone's deserving it or having to earn it.

heresy Christian belief that differs or deviates from the beliefs and standards as established by the ancient Christian Church in its councils. A person believing in a heresy is a heretic.

indentured servant a person who becomes the servant of another person for a specified period of time in return for a previously granted price. It was common practice in centuries past for individuals to agree to a period of years as an indentured servant in return for passage from Europe to the United States.

indulgence in Roman Catholic thought, a Christian may receive remission of punishment for a sin through the intervention of the church. Protestants rejected the idea of indulgences.

laypeople those members of the church other than the relatively small number of people set apart and ordained to full-time ministerial tasks.

liturgy the order of worship of a Christian church. Liturgy may often takes very different forms in different churches.

nonsectarian those things upon which all Christians agree, as opposed to those unique ideas (sectarian beliefs) that a particular group adopts and which are often used to identify it.

patroon term used among early Dutch colonial settlers to signify a person of leadership or authority.

presbytery among Presbyterians, who do not have bishops, churches are grouped into districts under the leadership of elders (in Greek, *presbyters*), hence a presbytery.

Purgatory Roman Catholics believe that Christians, before entering heaven, spend time in this intermediate realm, where they undergo further purification so they may enter heaven as sanctified (holy) individuals. Protestants rejected the idea of purgatory as nonbiblical.

Reformation the Reformation of the 16th century was the period of the formation and establishment of the Protestant movement, so-called because Protestants saw themselves as reforming the Christian church under the authority of the Bible.

relic Roman Catholics believe that objects associated with a holy person (such as body parts or articles of clothing) in some manner share in that person's holiness and may be used as objects of veneration by individuals who seek to improve their relationship with God. Protestants rejected the value of relics in the religious life.

revival a time of renewal of one's faith. Among Protestants, it has been common to organize special religious activities that focus on such renewal.

sacrament acts that are believed to specially manifest and dramatize the activities of God and are a special conduit of God's grace to the believer. Roman Catholics recognize seven sacraments, while Protestants recognize only two (Baptism and the Eucharist).

schism a break in the Christian communion, usually referring to a group of Christians who withdraw from one church and reorganize independently.

secular that which is not overtly religious. It is common in the modern world to divide one's existence into the sacred (having to do with God and faith) and secular (having to do with earthly, everyday affairs).

synod an governing council commonly consisting of the ministers and priests in a particular district or region.

theology the systematic presentation of one's beliefs. The creation of a theology is commonly seen as an activity carried out by the more intellectually qualified among the churches' leaders.

predestination the belief that God, being all-knowing and all-powerful, has already foreseen how people will ultimately act and hence has predestined some to experience salvation and some to be denied entrance into God's kingdom.

transubstantiation an understanding of the eucharistic sacrament which believes that once the proper words are spoken in the worship service, the essence of the elements of bread and wine become the essence of Jesus Christ, though outwardly appearances remain the same. Protestants uniformly rejected this understanding of the sacrament, although they were unable to reach a consensus on an alternate view.

TIME LINE

1607   The first Anglican Church is established at Jamestown, Virginia, under the leadership of chaplain John Hunt.

1623   Marble Collegiate Church is organized in New Amsterdam as a congregation of the Dutch Reformed Church in America. It is the oldest Protestant church in North America, with continuous service for more than 370 years.

1630   Puritans (Congregationalists) land in Massachusetts.

1638   The first Lutheran minister in America, Reorus Torkillus, arrives with Swedish settlers in what is now Delaware. In New Jersey, Francis Makemie arrives to begin organizing Presbyterianism in the colonies.

1740s   The First Great Awakening occurs in the American colonies.

1787   William White and Samuel Provoost travel to England to be consecrated as the first American Anglican bishops. They return to America to help found the Episcopal Church.

1789   Congress adopts the Constitution, whose First Amendment guarantees the free exercise of religion in the United States and separation of church and state.

1810   American Protestant concern for foreign missions is initially organized in the American Board of Commissioners for Foreign Missions, founded by Congregationalist leaders.

1852   Antoinette Brown, ordained by the Congregationalist Church, is the first woman ordained as a minister by American Protestants.

1925   The Scopes trial in Dayton, Tennessee, focuses national attention and debate on evolution in America's Protestant churches.

1957   The Congregational-Christian Churches and the Evangelical and Reformed Church merge to form the United Church of Christ.

1983   Separated since the Civil War, the two main branches of Presbyterians— the United Presbyterian Church in the U.S.A. and the Presbyterian Church in the United States—merge to form the Presbyterian Church (USA).

1988   The Lutheran Church in America, the American Lutheran Church, and the Association of Evangelical Lutheran Churches unite to form the Evangelical Lutheran Church in America.

1997   The Evangelical Lutheran Church votes pulpit and sacramental fellowship with the Presbyterian Church (USA), the United Church of Christ, and the Reformed Church in America.

RESOURCES

Reading List

Brown, Stephen F., *Protestantism* (World Religions Series). New York: Facts On File, 2002.

Carroll, Bret E., and Mark C. Carr, *The Routledge Historical Atlas of Religion in America* (Routledge Atlases of American History). Boston: Routledge, 2001.

Gaustad, Edwin Scott, *A Religious History of America*. San Francisco: HarperSanFrancisco, 2002.

Jacobsen, Douglas, and William Vance Trollinger, eds., *Re-Forming the Center: American Protestantism, 1900 to the Present*. Grand Rapids, Mich.: William. B. Eerdmans Publishing Co., 1998.

Marty, Martin E., ed., *Protestantism in the United States*. New York: Charles Scribner's Sons, 1986.

Noll, Mark, et al, eds. *Eerdman's Handbook to Christianity in America*. Grand Rapids, Mich.: William B. Eerdmans Publishing Company, 1983.

Williams, Peter. *America's Religions: From Their Origins to the Twenty-First Century*. Urbana, Ill.: University of Illinois Press, 2001.

Resources on the Web

The Protestant Reformation
history.hanover.edu/early/prot.html
Provides links to a variety of documents concerning the origin and early history of the Protestant movement.

Evangelical Lutheran Church in America
www.elca.org
Provides the history and an overview of the present program of one of the largest Protestant churches in America.

Presbyterian Church (USA)
www.pcusa.org
Official site of America's largest Protestant body with a number of links to the church's history, affiliates, and present activities.

United Church of Christ
www.ucc.org
Site for the largest church continuing the Congregationalist tradition.

Reformed Church in America
www.rca.org
Official site of the continuing Dutch Reformed Church in the United States.

Episcopal Church
www.episcopalchurch.org
The Episcopal Church's site includes links to Anglicanism worldwide.

National Council of Churches
ncccusa.org
Most of the larger Protestant Churches are members of the NCC and work with and through its many cooperating agencies.

INDEX

Note: *Italic* page numbers refer to illustrations.